From Uncertainty to Influence

FROM UNCERTAINTY
TO INFLUENCE

A Woman's Journey Through Challenge to Growth

BERTHA YENWO

SPEARS BOOKS
Denver, Colorado

Spears Books
An Imprint of Spears Media Press LLC
7830 W. Alameda Ave, Suite 103-247
Denver, CO 80226
United States of America

First Published in the United States of America in 2025 by Spears Books
www.spearsbooks.org
info@spearsmedia.com
Information on this title: www.spearsbooks.org/from-uncertainty-to-influence

ISBN: 9781957296593 (Paperback)
ISBN: 9781957296609 (Hardback)
Also available in Kindle & Google Books

Spears Media Press has no responsibility for the persistence or accuracy of urls for
external or third-party internet websites referred to in this publication, and does not
guarantee that any content on such websites is, or will remain, accurate or appropriate.

Designed and typeset by Spears Media Press LLC
Cover design: D. Kambem

Distributed globally by African Books Collective (ABC)
www.africanbookscollective.com

Contents

* * *

Acknowledgements

I used to think that for anyone to write a book, one just had to explain what he or she had in mind to the writer, and the writer would put everything down. With this mindset, I knew I just had to explain myself very well to the writer of my book. To my greatest surprise, I was told I had to write my story. I learnt this lesson the hard way, so I had to sit down and write out my thoughts. I also realised that the message you carry could be affected by the mindset you hold at the time you want to deliver it.

I started explaining my leadership journey to a friend who is a writer. I conveyed everything with pain and anger about what I had experienced as a leader. I was filled with bitterness and anguish. I continued to narrate my story from a negative perspective. The actions of some individuals during my leadership journey led me to develop a very poor perception and judgment of people, resulting in a lack of faith in them. This friend was so embarrassed that I was sharing such bitterness about the people I had worked with. He did not understand why I felt such bitterness towards them as a leader. I was uncomfortable with his viewpoint, and my response at that moment was to abandon the idea of writing this book.

Then I went to another person, a writer, for a second opinion. After listening to my story, he cautioned me first to consider the positive aspects of what I had done and to view my negative feelings as challenges. He pointed out my strengths and the good results I had achieved, despite my bitterness towards some of my followers. I thought that after hearing my thorough explanation of my accomplishments, he would begin writing my book. Unfortunately, he told me that it was my story and that I was the one responsible for writing it down. I paused the project for some time, but later gathered the courage to start writing again. Through his guidance, a plan and a book emerged that we have today.

From this story, I would like to extend my gratitude to everyone who contributed a word during the writing of this book, especially to Pa Buma Kor Dickson for igniting my writing spirit. Through your ideas, I learned to maintain a positive mindset about people. Your commitment and guidance, along with your careful analysis and appreciation of my activities, boosted my spirits and enabled me to organise all the ideas. Because of my fear of disappointing you, I became accountable for my story.

To all Nso women in Yaounde, especially the members of the Nsobati Women's Association, known in this book as the Women's Group, I learned and discovered so much about my attitude from you. You have all been great actors in my leadership journey. Your actions helped me read and master leadership principles and processes. Being with you provided me with both the opportunities and challenges of a leader, which formed my leadership story.

To my circle of strong men and women, my family and

friends, thank you for your incredible love, guidance, and support. You have been the compass and the light of this journey.

FROM UNCERTAINTY
TO INFLUENCE

ONE

Introduction

* * *

Lena is not just a leader; she is a force for transformation. Born and raised in Cameroon, she has spent decades shaping lives, breaking barriers, and redefining what is possible. Her journey has been anything but conventional, marked by trials that would have silenced many. Yet, she emerged with a philosophy that has guided her every step.

"Create Something, Own Something through Excellence"

From the depths of adversity, she built a life of purpose, leadership and influence. She has faced rejection, humiliation and manipulation. She has battled poverty, not just as an economic condition, but as a mindset that seeks to limit potential. And yet through it all, Lena has refused to be defined by circumstances. Instead, she has used them as fuel to rise.

Her unrelenting pursuit of knowledge has taken her across the continents, learning from the best, refining her skills, and earning recognition from world-class institutions. As an educator, mentor, speaker and motivator, she has touched thousands of lives, imparting wisdom that has helped many navigate their own leadership journeys. Her presence is not just seen, but also felt in boardrooms, classrooms, on global platforms, and in the hearts of those who have drawn strength from her resilience.

But how did she get here? What shaped the woman who now stands as a beacon of excellence and empowerment? Was it talent, sheer determination, or something more?

This book is the answer. It is a journey into the making of a leader, the struggles, triumphs, and defining moments that turned obstacles into stepping stones. Through her challenges and experiences, Lena shares her story and crafts a blueprint for effective leadership. She reveals the everyday struggles that leaders face and, more importantly, how to overcome them. It is a call to those who dare to dream, seek to lead, and refuse to settle for anything less than excellence.

Lena's story is more than inspiration; it is an invitation to step beyond limitations, to embrace the power of transformation, and to craft a legacy of impact.

The question is, are you ready to take this journey with her?

If so, she invites you to take a moment, gather your thoughts, and prepare yourself for this inspiring journey.

Here's how it all started....

It started in 1956 in a small village called Mbveh, located in Kumbo, Bui Division of the Northwest Region of Cameroon. This village is known for its hospitality and communal spirit. The people are well-behaved, and everyone loves each other. There was no such appellation as "my mother" at all. Most females who had given birth were called mothers of all the children in the community. As a result, children were regarded as the offspring of every woman in the village. Women cared for the children of others as if they were theirs. Sharing food and drink with the needy was not a big thing at all. Women and men rallied to educate themselves, and the young ones without difficulty. In fact, the village was a haven for many. Even when you go to the city, nostalgia unconsciously draws you back to the village. Stories about the hospitality had transcended to other villages that could not resist but sent envoys to visit and copy our lifestyle, which was later inculcated into their villages. Everything was going on well till one fateful day, a conflict erupted between the royal and Deng families, which resulted in the deaths of numerous members of both families. During the period of the fight, Mrs. Lulu Anna was heavily pregnant. As a strong lady, she gave birth to a bouncy baby girl named after the crisis by Mr. Lulu as **Yigolalena**–Who then will survive?

Mr. Lulu was afraid that his wife and daughter could be killed, so he fled with them to a nearby village for safety. He only returned with his family after the crisis had ended. As a fervent Catholic Christian, Mr. Lulu and his wife, Anna, went for the child's dedication. During the dedication, the parish priest, who hailed from Holland, was unable to pronounce the name, Yigolalena, so he simplified it to "Lena" and baptised the child as such. A few years after Lena's christening, her father was recognised with a traditional title for his talents and skills in bringing people together.

As a titleholder, he consequently created a large community of friends and families who were passionate practitioners of their culture. Lena's life story began in this community.

Even as a child, Lena was eager to watch and admire everything happening around her. She enjoyed serving the many family members who attended family gatherings at their compound. Every evening, she played with friends before fetching water for her grandmother, Yaya Sheila. She joined the church women for morning services daily, especially on Sundays. Her mother, Anna, was responsible for the church keys—opening and closing the church every morning and evening. Lena and her friends attended doctrinal classes at this church, which was located near her home.

Lena attended the Catholic Primary School a few miles away from her home. She began breeding the spirit of sociality by making friends with her schoolmates, Beatrice, Electa, Lilian, Grace, Irene, Emma, Esther, Rosemary, and Tina. They all shared stories and meals in school. The only language spoken in school was Lamnso', their mother tongue. As friends from the same neighbourhood, they trekked every morning together to cover the long distance from their houses to school. Adjacent to the primary school was a gigantic church where all the people of the Catholic faith in Kumbo converged every Sunday for prayers. At that time, it was interesting to see that only the white priests from Italy and Holland could deliver church sermons because there were no black priests at the time.

While in Class Five, the teacher appointed Lena as the head girl. Morning masses were compulsory for all the primary pupils, and classes started immediately after the mass and ended in the afternoons at 2:30 pm. Lena was in charge of the school choir, which sang every morning in church. Choir practice occurred every Wednesday of the week. Every Thursday, the Class Five girls were sent to the domestic science teacher's home to wash clothes and dishes. Lena would caution her friends to wash the clothes and dishes carefully because Madam Domii (nickname of the Domestic Science teacher crafted by the pupils) was very strict and harsh. If anything happened to her dishes, she would thrash or sanction the pupil seriously, and she could report the particular pupil to her parents, who would again punish her without even wanting to know what happened. On those same Thursdays, the Class Five boys stayed in class for manual arts, a subject Lena did not master then. On other days, pupils were organised in groups to work in the school garden, while others were assigned to harvest coffee at the headmaster's farm. This was a very interesting exercise for the pupils. They considered it a duty and privilege, and no one complained. At that time, it was about obedience and respect. No child was punished by a parent for coming home late on such a day. Every day, after classes, girls and boys played dodgeball and football before rushing back to their different homes.

When Lena completed her primary education, she enrolled at the only Catholic secondary school, Saint Augustine's College, located at Mboh-Mbim in Kumbo. As a college student, she made many friends and interacted with boys and girls from neighbouring towns with different backgrounds and cultures. Lena learned to speak English and Pidgin English with her friends. She could no longer speak her mother tongue because it was unacceptable and punishable. It was shameful to hear someone speaking in their mother tongue. In Form Three, she encountered many incidents that contributed to the rapid change in her life. While in Form Four, she became the sports prefect of the school. During this time, she led her school team to the inter-city competition games, where her school emerged victorious.

The distance between Mbveh quarters and Mboh-Mbim was significant, and there were no township taxis available at that time in Kumbo. Lena and her friends would trek to Mboh-Mbim village two weeks before school reopened. They carried their books, foodstuffs, mattresses, and belongings themselves from their different destinations to Mboh-Mbim.

After completing her secondary school studies at St Augustine's, she left her village to further her studies at a high school in Kumba, a town in the Southwest Region of Cameroon. She was admitted to the College of Arts and Sciences, Kumba, where she encountered a new subject called *economics*. During her secondary school days, students were given the impression that economics was a subject for boys, and girls had an obligation to study domestic science. They were not allowed to read economics. This notion did not have a place in this high school in Kumba, as she discovered that the subject of economics was open to whoever had an interest. She then took it as a challenge to study the subject, and some friends helped her to master it so well. Her friend Francisca lived with her at the National High School Street near Hausa quarters. As friends, they would trek from this street through the railway station at Mabanda village to Buea Road, where the high school was located. Walking together was always fun, allowing them to talk about their lives and experiences. There were no township taxis then.

During high school, she realised that life in a day school differed from what she had experienced in her boarding school. She noticed that boys and girls of single-sex boarding secondary schools had their own ways of interacting with other students, unlike students who came from mixed-sex boarding secondary schools. Some boys from single-sex boarding secondary schools loved hanging out together and were always fond of bullying girls. In this high school, student clubs like Alpha Club and

Venus Club were created to promote student solidarity. Club members were all students from different cultures and backgrounds. These club activities brought a lot of discrimination and class stratification, instead of unity and solidarity among students. Members of some clubs, like the Alpha club, were not allowed to meet and greet other students who were not members of their club. Some members of a few clubs were so proud and arrogant and tended to look down on some students.

After grasping rich knowledge in high school, her family celebrated her traditional and civil service wedding, after which she left for another town known as Yaounde in the Centre Region, Cameroon. While in Yaounde, she enrolled as a student in the only university at the time, the University of Yaounde. There were no guidance counsellors to orient students on career options. With the assistance of Richard Tang, a senior student whom she had known back in secondary school, she registered as a private law student at the Faculty of Law and Economics of this university.

At Yaounde University, classes were always full before 8 am, especially in the Amphitheatre 700, and one had to leave home very early to have a seat. While at the university, Lena met many friends and classmates from her former schools because the University of Yaounde was the only university in the country at the time. They all became friends again, and there was no discrimination amongst friends as in high school. Because they all came from a purely English-speaking background, they faced a particular difficulty: mastery of the French language. They had several academic challenges and were obliged to form reading groups and clubs that enabled them to study. Despite that, Lena's school performance for the first academic year was terrific. She succeeded in moving to the next academic year and gave birth to a baby girl that same year. She was one of the students who spent four years in this faculty to obtain a first degree because, after a serious student strike, an administrative decision was taken, and the number of years for obtaining a degree in the law faculty was reduced from four to three years. After completing her first degree in English private law, she took a few public examinations but did not succeed. She became so demoralised, and when she was about to give up, the government announced the recruitment of first-degree holders to work as contract officers in the civil service. Lena was one of those recruited to work with the Ministry of Justice. She was first posted to work with the Ministry of Justice in Buea, in the Southwest Region of Cameroon. She worked there for a year and was transferred back to Yaounde for family reasons.

When she returned to Yaounde, she was sent to work at the Court of First Instance. While there, Lena had a challenge as she was working with magistrates, her schoolmates in the Faculty of Law who had succeeded in public examinations and trained as magistrates. She knew very well that she did not want to be a magistrate or a lawyer, even though she read law and obtained a law degree. She kept convincing herself about her intellectual weakness and believed she wasn't good at public speaking.

In her mind, Lena imagined her inability to be a magistrate and, at the same time, not being happy with her job at the Court of First Instance. It was boring routine work. She then requested to be transferred from the Court of First Instance to the Ministry of Justice. While in the Ministry of Justice, she was tasked with preparing retirement decisions for state agents. Lena was happy with the tasks because she could reflect on the issues, study the different cases, and make proposals to the Director of Human Resources. The work was enjoyable, and she worked with much enthusiasm. While in that office, she met four colleagues of French-speaking background preparing for public competitive examinations. From them, Lena learned how to prepare for competitive examinations. Mr. Datchoua particularly trained her on how to tackle examination questions effectively. With this new knowledge and motivation, she wrote the competitive examination for the National School of Administration and Magistracy (ENAM) and succeeded after several years of failed attempts.

While in the School of Administration and Magistracy, she read Administrative Law and graduated as a tax inspector in 1993. She was posted to work under the Ministry of Finance at the Department of Taxation. She worked there as the chief auditor of taxes for several years and as head of tax centre number seven. She learned how to manage human, material, and financial resources. She retired from the civil service in 2016 as a sub-director of stamp duty for the Department of Taxation.

As a retired person, she devised a vision to inculcate values in young people from their early ages through a school she created known as the Mike Denny Institute of Excellence. The Institute is about quality education for quality pupils and students; it emphasizes cultivating the culture of excellence in young people so that they can make a difference in their lives and become better citizens.

TWO

The Birth of the Dream

* * *

Kumbo boasts a vibrant market that operates once a week, attracting traders from nearby villages and towns. It is the only venue where the people of this town gather to sell their farm products and connect with friends and loved ones. The circulation of money was limited, except on these market days. Most of the men, who were coffee farmers then, sold coffee, kola nuts, and livestock such as cows, fowl, and goats. Women, for their part, sold potatoes, beans, cocoyam, maize, and beverages like corn beer. People from neighbouring cities also came to sell clothing, farm equipment, and various items such as dishes and building materials. In exchange, they purchased foodstuffs like potatoes, beans, fowl, and goats for consumption or resale in their own towns. An essential item that should not be overlooked at the market is palm wine, predominantly consumed by the men who frequented the market. As a result of the business and palm wine drinking, market days became days for social interaction, leisure, entertainment and tourism.

It is fair to say that commerce was merely a secondary activity because the primary endeavours of these people during that time were agriculture and hunting. Farming was primarily performed by women, while men engaged in hunting. The farmers grew crops such as coffee, maize, beans, cocoyam, potatoes, cassava, and vegetables. The harvest season was particularly vibrant in the Kumbo community, as it fostered harmony among the residents; men and young boys from different families typically gathered in large numbers to assist the women in transporting farm produce from the fields to their homes.

Talking about religion, the most prominent denomination in Kumbo is the Roman Catholic church. There are also Muslims, Presbyterians, and Baptists. Going to church early in the mornings was a way of life for the people of Kumbo. Men, women, and children trekked long distances to attend morning masses or Stations of the Cross during the Lenten season. Sundays were special days for women, as they stayed in the church premises for their meetings. The early Christian women, fondly called *a mami fourteen*, had made it an obligation for most women in this community to embrace the Catholic faith. They criticised the pagan way of life and rejected the idea of traditional chiefs marrying off young girls. These women used songs to protest the injustices perpetrated by the traditional rulers of this community. The songs were also a means of expressing their feelings about unfavourable decisions against women. Interestingly, these songs became their primary tool for correcting, protesting, appreciating, or approving what they believed was right or wrong.

Regarding education, most primary schools in Kumbo are denominational schools run by Catholics, Presbyterians, and Baptist missionaries. Some primary schools in Kumbo, especially in the hinterlands, were constructed by the government without benches for pupils to sit on. In most of these schools, children sat on bare floors to study.

The education of children is supposed to be the responsibility of both parents, but this is not the case in Kumbo, where Christian women, especially Catholic women, have made their children's education a priority and, at times, have done so solely. On Sundays, they come together in groups to meet, share ideas, and discuss the education of their children. This initiative was instituted by Rev. Father John Kolkman.

Although most people in Kumbo are Christians, they love their culture deeply—a culture of solidarity. Both men and women believe in their traditions. They share a common cultural heritage. They enjoy singing and dancing and often organise traditional ceremonies for birth, marriage, and death within the community. The people take pride in performing and showcasing their strengths through masquerades that are presented by men. Young boys live under the care and responsibility of their parents until they reach the age of eighteen. A young boy can only leave his parents' home after building his own house. A young girl leaves her parents' home to enter marriage. With the advent of Christianity and its system of education, the traditional roles of both boys and girls changed drastically.

Focusing on the women's lives in Kumbo, we see that they worked very hard yet lived in poverty. Their only occupation was subsistence farming. Encapsulated by a hilly landscape, these women will go long distances to farm in valleys and marshy areas. These women worked very hard, but their output was not usually much because of the nature of the farmlands. They must toil on several pieces of land to produce enough for consumption and sale. Consequently, they were obliged to cultivate several pieces of land in different villages to produce more food and have better yields. In some areas, the women faced problems of cattle destroying their crops. The head of the traditional council was constantly preoccupied with settling disputes between women and cattle owners, mostly the Mbororos. These herders went with their cows around the farmlands in search of pasture, which often ended up causing severe damage to crops, creating many problems among community dwellers. Though farming was the central preoccupation of the people of Kumbo, the farmers lacked farm tools and good roads for carrying their farm products to the markets. Women carried out subsistence farming for their immediate consumption. There were no agricultural technicians to assist them in growing their crops.

Young girls were obliged to accompany their mothers to the farms. A young girl was expected to walk long distances to any of the farms, depending on the wishes and decisions of her mother, without complaining. After afternoon classes, a girl in primary school had to fetch firewood and harvest vegetables for the evening meals. Going to fetch water from the stream was the job of young girls, and young boys spent their time playing with their friends. Mothers tolerated the laziness of boys, but girls were never given a breathing space. Some boys spent their time in the palace running after masquerades. Because of poverty or lack of money, many young girls dropped out of school, some went wayward and gave birth to babies at a tender age.

Muslim families did not like to send their children to school, even though there were no Muslim schools by then. Muslim parents preferred to send their children to sell clothing and articles in the market or foodstuffs along the street. Muslim girls were encouraged to carry out commerce and get themselves ready for marriage instead of going to school.

Diverting to health, people had to trek long distances to the two main hospitals built by the missionaries. There were no health centres in the hinterlands. People were not educated on the importance of their health, and some did not see the need to go to the hospital. Women were always occupied with educating their children and running their homes rather than taking care of themselves. People went to hospitals only when they were seriously ill.

Traditionally, in this environment, some girls were whisked off into marriages at a tender age. Some families still did not see the importance of education for a girl child. Those who continued schooling were primarily interested in teaching and nursing, so we had many people, especially women, as teachers and nurses. Very few girls ventured into the technical and management fields like finance and engineering because girls were not encouraged to study the science subjects. Studying subjects like mathematics and physics seemed difficult for most girls. When Lena brought a family member from Kumbo to Yaounde in the nineties, the child was always demoted to a lower class. After serious investigations from the community, she was made to understand that several private individuals had opened schools in most villages in Kumbo with no qualified teachers. In some of the nursery schools, children were taken care of by young girls with no educational qualifications.

As concerns people living with disabilities in Kumbo town, they are hardly seen outside their homes. They do not sit along the streets to beg from passers-by because that is not the culture of the people. They are never taken to church or for any ceremonies. They do not mingle with other people in the community.

Because these categories of people are not seen on the streets, no one believed they existed in this community. No one cared about these people with disabilities. The burden of caring for them fell on their family members, especially their mothers. Pa Humprey has been living with a disability for several years, and his wife, Mami Vero, has been the breadwinner of the family. Mami Ben had a son who had never left his bed since birth. Mami Ben carried him on his back wherever she went.

Because of the difficulties in Kumbo, most women and men found themselves in cosmopolitan towns like Yaounde, Douala, Limbe, and Bafoussam for greener pastures. Some came to Yaounde as students, others as job seekers, some as business-men and women, and many young boys for military services, who in turn brought their wives from the villages to the cities.

Most students who left the villages for the University of Yaounde after obtaining their Advanced Level certificates had enrolled for university studies without any knowledge or ori-entation about the careers and professions necessary for them. They had no one to guide them on such issues.

By 1998, the population of the Kumbo community in Yaounde had grown, and they needed a community hall for their monthly meetings and cultural celebrations. The cultural meetings were held in people's homes. As the group grew, it became difficult for one person to host all the members in his home. There was no space for children to play or dance, as it was the tradition and purpose of the coming together.

Growing up in Kumbo and being conscious of these difficul-ties and challenges in this community was so demotivating and discouraging. As a young girl in this community, Lena did not like going to the farm. She went to the farm only out of respect, love, and obedience to her mother. Each time she went to the farm, she always wished the clock would spin quickly for her to return home. During her secondary school days, she spent all the holidays going to the farm, and going back to school after the holidays was so exciting. She was always pleased because she had to return to meet all her dormitory friends.

Lena witnessed the difficulties faced by women in her community. She would pity them because their only activities were going to their farms, the church, and the market.

While in high school in Kumba, she started developing the desire to help the women of her community have better lives. Whenever she thought of her mother and other women of Kumbo, who themselves were not educated but did everything they could to educate their children from the proceeds obtained from their farm products, she kept wondering and dreaming of how she would one day help them. She recalled how once in her secondary school days, she was sent away from school for not completing her school fees of fifty thousand francs (CFA). Her mother sold ten tins of beans at six thousand francs each and raised the money for her sake, enabling her to return to school. Her mother continued to play a vital role in her education. The thought of how she would ever pay her back and show her some appreciation never left her mind, but unfortunately, her mother passed on to eternity, and Lena never fulfilled this dream.

As a civil servant in Yaounde, she started visiting the different cultural and development groups of Kumbo residents in Yaounde. She encountered many women who had abandoned the pursuit of education because they had to travel to this big city to meet their husbands. Lena had several conversations with some who had left the villages for the big towns or cities for babysitting and home management jobs. She recognised some elderly women who had left the villages because they preferred the good life in the cities rather than what they had in the villages. Lena also came across friends, former schoolmates, and senior women who had made it in life and had maximum satisfaction as employees in the civil service and as housewives.

Her love for her community and the thought of giving back continued to grow, and her dream of helping, especially women, have better lives grew from strength to strength. She started carving out ways to solve some of the community's problems. Lena began rallying people, raising awareness, and mobilising some close friends to solve some of these problems. She came up with the idea of women coming together to form a united front for sharing and exchanging ideas for a positive change of mindset, a change in their lives, and the community.

In 1996, she invited a group of twenty-five women from Kumbo, now residents of Yaounde, for a brief meeting. They all met at Mrs. Tekere's house, where her husband was the head of the Kumbo community in Yaounde. She shared her plans to create a group with the purpose of unity. She made them understand they could achieve great things for their community by coming together. They could solve personal problems and support one another because they were far from home. They could always gather to assist each other in times of difficulty. She highlighted the possibilities of teaching their cultural values and traditions to their children through such gatherings. The women listened to her and clapped to acknowledge and appreciate the idea. Some women sang traditional songs, and everyone was pleased with the proposal. There were shouts of joy and exchanges of handshakes, especially with Lena, the initiator.

An idea for the women to unite for the development of their community was born. A group, known as the *Women's Group*, was launched on June 9, 1996, to promote unity, solidarity, and the development of women and their community.

THREE

The Mission of the Dream

* * *

Community problems are local issues that can only be solved by engaging the people of the communities. They also require support from other stakeholders, like governments, corporate partners, nonprofit organisations, or individuals. To understand community problems, they must first of all be identified and analysed. This will enable people to better understand their problems for better solutions. It is said that you never solve a problem for a person without the person. You must let the person recognise the problem, but Lena and her team immediately started implementing her dream. She devised several ideas and solutions to empower people, build capacities and raise awareness on these community issues.

SOLUTIONS TO THE PROBLEMS

When people are empowered, it changes the way they see the world, increases their capacities, changes the way they interact with others, and changes their way of thinking. Engaging in community activities should make life better for people in the community. Lena and her team embarked on making their own contributions and finding solutions to the difficulties faced by the people of this community. They changed people's mindsets in different areas like health care, poverty alleviation, education, vulnerable people, community infrastructures, agriculture, and environmental sustainability.

Contributions to Health Problems

In 2002, as the President of the Women's Group based in Yaounde, Lena and the team organised several health screening activities in Yaounde. In 2006, three hundred women who lived in Yaounde were screened for cervical cancer with the assistance of the United Nations Population Fund. In 2011, Lena initiated a wellness program known as *Kitukem* to promote healthy living for women in Kumbo and Yaounde. Many women found this valuable and appreciated this program. Consequently, educating women about their health during their monthly meetings became a practice. In 2014, Lena mobilised women for the fight against teenage pregnancies in Kumbo, and one hundred and thirty students from ten schools were trained and given educational talks against teenage pregnancies. Sporting activities became so interesting for women that they became a way of keeping fit and maintaining healthy bodies.

Contributions to the Problems of Poverty
Diversification of Agricultural activities

To help rural women diversify their farming or agricultural activities, Lena created a group called *Bongabaa Bayam-Sellam Women's Group* (BBSW), which later became a Women's Farmers' Cooperative. The creation of this group had the objective of helping women to alleviate poverty and increase production. The women started cultivating varieties of vegetables like green beans, carrots, tomatoes, cabbages, onions, ginger, and garlic that could fetch them fast and much money in addition to cultivating maize, potatoes, beans, cassava, and cocoyams. Today's women believe that the commercialisation of potatoes and beans has boosted their children's education and empowered them financially.

Another project, *One Woman a Bag of Fertiliser for the Rural Women*, was also created to enable women to buy their farm inputs at affordable prices. A bag of fertiliser used to cost 19,000 frs (Nineteen thousand francs CFA) at that time. Lena pleaded with some of the community's elites and businesspeople, who agreed to support the women by subsidising the extra 9,000 frs (nine thousand francs) per bag. At the end of January of each year, every member of the Bongabaa Bayam-Sellam Women's Cooperative paid 10,000 frs (ten thousand francs) for a bag of fertiliser. The coordinator of the cooperative was in charge of collecting the money from all members every month of January. She ensured that the total quantity of fertiliser requested by members was bought and distributed.

These women farmers also initiated another project to buy other farm inputs like insecticides, watering cans, etc., through their personal contributions, which boosted their agricultural activities.

Some school drop-out boys, in order to alleviate poverty, decided to engage themselves in agricultural activities. In 2008, Lena created this group known as the *Friends and Builders' Farmers Group*, which later became the Farmers' Cooperative. This group, which started with twenty-five members, kept increasing, and by 2016, the group had grown to four hundred members. With the advent of the crisis in the area, some members were kidnapped, some lost their lives, and some moved to other regions. Those who stayed back in the village still carry out their agricultural activities as a source of living.

Creation of Social Ventures

Lena initiated a financial scheme for women in 2013, the Women's Trust Fund, which was legalised as a financial cooperative in 2022. Under this scheme, members are granted small loans to manage their business activities. The Women's Group has several self-help groups whose objectives are for women to financially support each other in promoting their business activities with the goal of achieving financial independence.

To strengthen women's financial abilities, Lena initiated several saving schemes to promote the culture of savings, like the Tasban Plan, Children's Fund, Christmas Fund, Solidarity Fund, Condolence Fund, Development Fund, One Woman-One Account Saving scheme, and My Purse. The Buying and Selling of Basic Needs scheme was also created to enable women to have their basic needs, like washing soap, salt, rice, groundnut oil, palm oil, seasoning cubes, and matches, at affordable prices.

Several trainings and workshops were organised to enhance women's capacities in financial literacy and financial management, especially the workshops conducted by the Africa Dream Group and Union Farms from Buea. This training enabled the women to strengthen their skills in keeping good financial records and cultivating vegetables.

Contributions to Educational Problems

Regarding education, Lena invited fifteen young girls from the Universities of Yaounde I and II to her office in Yaounde in 2014. During their discussions, they all discovered that back in their secondary school days, they had escaped from studying mathematics. Some of the girls disclosed their hatred for this subject at that time. Through investigations within the community, Lena understood that there was a problem with the learning of mathematics by young girls in Kumbo. They all agreed that it was necessary to help other young girls change their mindsets. A group known as Girls for Change (GFC) was created to support and promote the study of Science, Technology, Engineering, and Mathematics. The Girls for Change Association continued to conduct sensitisation campaigns on the need for young girls to study STEM subjects. Several campaigns were carried out on the issue in Kumbo and Muslim schools.

Concerning the case of unqualified teachers in the Kumbo community, Lena went to the Divisional Delegation of the Ministry of Basic Education in Kumbo to get an insight into the story. Together with the Divisional Delegate, they devised a strategy of giving educational assistance to the nursery and primary school teachers to upgrade their education standards. An association, Nso Nursery and Primary School Teachers' Vision (NNPST-VISION), comprised of nursery and primary school teachers, was created.

To help students choose better future careers, Lena initiated a group in 2012 known as the Nkumbiwa Development Forum to guide and counsel students of the rural communities after obtaining their advanced level certificates to choose better professional careers. This group took it as a duty to always go back to the villages in Kumbo during the months of July and August of every year to meet these youths for the orientation seminars before they entered the different universities for further studies.

In partnership with the Ministry of Arts and Culture, the members of this group organised a book fair to promote the culture of reading and the importance of building libraries in schools. By exhibiting the works and images of these famous writers of Bui Division, the group wanted to encourage and motivate the youth to understand and realise the importance of education and its impact on each citizen.

Adult literacy enhancement became a continuous activity organised every month to uplift women who, for certain reasons, dropped out of school and those who never had the opportunity to go to school.

As the leader of the Women's Group, Lena initiated the study of Lamnso' among children and youths resident in Yaounde. Workshops on teaching the mother tongue to Kumbo youths and adults have been a continuous activity to date. This has been a way of helping all the children and parents to bond and connect to their roots.

Lena initiated several conflict resolution training workshops, which were carried out in the Kumbo and Jakiri communities. These workshops helped to solve the farmer-grazer problems faced by the women farmers. Through the amicable settlement of such problems, the women learned how to interact with the cattle owners, decreasing the farmer-grazer problems plaguing the community. These workshops aimed to educate rural women on the importance of peace and solidarity and how to prevent conflict.

In order to promote peace, unity, social cohesion, cultural

solidarity, and living together, the women always come together to celebrate and promote their culture through songs, dances, and other activities. They are the ones who spearhead cultural activities and the cultural jamborees. They enjoy speaking in their mother tongue and sharing and practising all the traditional values and customs peculiar to women of this community. Sometimes, little disputes are settled during these meetings, and food and drinks are shared with everyone without discrimination, whether they are Christians or Muslims. The women also enjoy celebrating their farm produce, like the Potato and Beans Festival, which is celebrated every month of July. This celebration promotes the continuous cultivation and commercialisation of beans and potatoes. There has also been continuous sensitisation of the effects of climate change.

Contributions to the Problems of Persons Living with Disabilities

In 2003, several persons living with disabilities in the Kumbo community were identified. Lena saw the need to bring these people together under one umbrella, and an association known as the Bui Disabled Persons' Association (BDPA) was created to cater to their needs. To assist this category of persons in alleviating poverty, a project known as *One Man, One Goat* was created to enable persons living with disabilities to generate income for themselves through the rearing of goats for commercial purposes. After brainstorming on how to carry out the project, investigations were carried out at the level of the villages in Kumbo to identify the right people to carry out the project. Some persons were contacted at the level of each village who purchased the animals that were distributed to the members of the Bui Disabled Persons' Association. Every year, the Women's

Group donates materials like washing soap, equipment, and several food items (rice, sugar, milk) to persons with disabilities. With support from the Ministry of Social Welfare and the First Lady's Foundation, the Bui Disabled Persons' Association (BDPA) members have benefited several times from the largess of the First Lady of Cameroon.

Lena personally carried out several sensitisation campaigns throughout Kumbo and the whole of Bui Division to educate the local population, especially the mayors and all the elites, about the necessity of promoting the rights of persons living with disabilities and supporting them to sustain their lives.

Contributions to Community Infrastructural Development

On the 18th of April 1998, Lena and her team mobilised all the people of the Kumbo community living in Yaounde for a fundraising event. Money was raised to buy a piece of land in Yaounde to construct a community hall. After three subsequent fundraising events organised by the women, the said piece of land was purchased, and the construction work for the hall started. As if this wasn't enough, in 2011, the women initiated another fundraising event known as "Operation Two Sheets of Zinc" for the roofing of this hall. The hall was completed in 2014, and today, there is a community hall for Kumbo community residents in Yaounde.

As the Women's Group leader, Lena came up with the idea of donating school benches to primary schools in the different villages of Kumbo. Lena and her team worked with some elites of the community and the Diaspora, and benches were made and distributed to fifty primary schools in Kumbo.

Lena also initiated the construction of an empowerment

centre for women, youths, and persons with disabilities in Jakiri. These groups will use this hall for their social and cultural activities. The centre has been completed and transferred to the Jakiri Council, a town in Bui Division.

Contributions to Environmental Sustainability

There has also been continuous sensitisation of the effects of climate change. Women were encouraged through several workshops to plant climate-friendly trees like tefrosia to promote soil fertility.

FOUR

The Impact of the Dream
The Change

* * *

Creating change in the community involves enforcing change in people's way of thinking, behaving, and doing things. Social ventures aim to change people's lives, create opportunities, and generate additional income, but the change is not always easy. The outcomes of Lena's activities and her team brought several changes to the community.

CREATING A CHANGE MINDSET

To change a community's mindset, we must help people understand themselves and their community. It is necessary to create awareness about community work. The people must see the problem for change to be effective. To create change, you must first bring everyone in the community to understand the need for change. All stakeholders should be aware and should work on a common agenda. Because of the several sensitisation campaigns that were carried out about the plight of persons living with disabilities and teenage pregnancies, many stakeholders like mayors, Senior Divisional Officers, civil servants from the Ministries of Education and Social Welfare, councillors, women, youths, Christians, and Muslims, became aware of these problems in the different communities.

This brought the birth of *new mindsets*, new ways of doing things, and new ways of living lives. People, especially those with disabilities, became aware of the new relationships with people. A new mindset of making people responsible for their lives started growing in the community.

The mindset of continuous dependence by women began changing. Men also started having faith in women's activities. Some men, especially the traditional rulers, started seeing the importance of educating the young girls.

Meetings and meeting houses became places for social gatherings, promoting social interaction, solidarity, bonding, networking, and consequently social cohesion. The community people enhanced their habits of always uniting with others, especially during sad and happy events.

Most health issues were easily discussed in different meeting houses. Health practitioners found out that it was easy for them to meet several women in a single place at short notice. Through the wellness programs, women now knew how to care for themselves regularly. Women took it as a duty to carry out their health checks every month of February before celebrating International Women's Day in March. Educative talks during meetings became of great importance as vaccination campaigns were carried out at the different meeting houses to convince the people to believe in the vaccinations. Women could then be seen taking their children spontaneously to hospitals for consultations and vaccination.

By interacting with each other, the women strengthened their social skills. Some learned to share their ideas, communicate, and express themselves fluently. The women also learned much about values like patience, tolerance, perseverance, commitment, discipline, love, and respect. The leaders of the different meeting groups and the members acquired new skills in planning and implementing their groups' goals and objectives.

With the influx of foreigners and interaction of people of different cultures, people started mingling with others in several ways, and new habits cropped up in the communities. For example, some people abandoned the English names for their children and French names like "DIEUDONNE," "RENE," and "ELVIS" became famous and rampant.

The interaction with businesspeople from other towns led to a change in people's behaviour in the community. The women learned how to communicate with non-natives while selling their farm products. It steered the spread of Pidgin English in the community, as many people learned to communicate with strangers in the language they best understood. We witnessed an increase in the variety of foods produced in the communities and a change in people's consumption patterns. People who used to eat mostly fufu and vegetables started consuming foods like "water fufu and eru," a new meal to them. People from other cities who came to buy potatoes, beans, and goats came in with different products like rice, fish, and groundnut oil to sell. Many women got involved in cassava production because the sale of garri (a product from the transformation of cassava) brought in a lot of money to the women farmers.

The interaction between people living with disabilities and other people in the community has also promoted an inclusive way of living, peace, love and harmony. The lives of people with disabilities changed because they became registered members of the social welfare centre managed by the state. They were given identification cards as persons living with disabilities. This helped boost their morale because with the cards, their children were given free education in government schools.

It was a time for innovation, as new concepts like unity and solidarity, climate change, and STEM education were introduced in the community. The notion of associations and cooperatives brought in new ideas that have contributed to a change in the community. Creating financial structures like poverty schemes, business schemes, thrift and loan schemes, and self-help groups was new to women.

The members of the Bongabaa Bayam-Sellam Women's Cooperative increased the cultivation of new products, and different vegetables like green beans, carrots, tomatoes, ginger, onions, garlic, cabbages, cassava flour, cassava starch, etc. Cultivating natural and organic farm products for sale also had a high demand because of the reduced use of fertilisers in production, generating additional income for women. The rearing of local poultry intensified and attracted buyers from other towns, which changed the farmers' lives.

Women were trained on new methods of farming to stop the slash-and-burn techniques and prevent soil erosion from occurring. The Friends and Builders Farmers' Cooperative began producing Nerica rice, which became a source of income and food for them. The Ministry of Agriculture supported this project through a training program for the cultivation of Nerica rice. The members of this cooperative were trained by the Riba Agro-Forestry company on how to plant economic forest trees like "njansang," etc, which can help to change the environment and bring more revenue to them. The Nkumbiwa Development Forum's planting of trees to protect the environment was a giant step. The **educational skills** acquired by the nursery and primary school teachers had some added value. They learned different ways of planning their schoolwork and managing their classrooms. The knowledge acquired helped them to be pedagogically up to date. Teachers' levels of teaching improved. They saw their individual performances change, and the teaching and learning standards of the different schools changed positively.

Another factor that changed the lives of primary school pupils was the provision of didactic materials and benches in schools. Some primary school pupils went from sitting and writing on bare floors to sitting and writing on benches. The training of students, primary school teachers and school dropouts in ICTs significantly improved the literacy level of the youth in this community.

Acquiring **financial skills** empowered many women to manage their economic activities. Women's incomes increased from the different financial structures created and the cultivation of organic farm products. Through the different capacity-building seminars and training workshops, more women acquired skills in financial literacy, entrepreneurship, leadership, marketing, and management of their farms, homes, and businesses.

Women learned to acquire assets by building social capital through crowdfunding, which brought about reciprocity and trust among members of the different groups. Women could acquire property and other durables that they would not have acquired if they had not been given such knowledge and assistance and had not been working together.

The communities witnessed an increase in **job creation,** as many jobs were created for a specific category of people in these communities. Many bike riders could be seen carrying foodstuffs from the farms to the markets. Many boys became middlemen in buying potatoes and beans on behalf of big buyers from other cities. Truck-pushing businesses intensified as truck pushers and loaders became very busy packaging and packing beans and potatoes into the big trucks for onward transportation to big cities. These boys became so occupied, and fewer boys were seen roaming the streets.

The increase in economic activities led to an increase in council revenue. The demand for stalls and stores from the council for the sale of agricultural foodstuffs and other products increased because the number of women selling in the market increased. Collecting market dues from different vendors and transporters increased the council revenue.

By inculcating the entrepreneurial spirit in women and young boys, they discovered great economic opportunities to excel in different business activities. Both men and women became very active on market days.

Due to the diversification of food production, agricultural activities increased. Most members of the different farmers' cooperatives embraced agricultural activities, and the groups kept growing from strength to strength. By commercialising their farm products, all the members acquired additional income and consequently changed their lives.

COLLECTIVE LEADERSHIP

Community problems need collective leadership. Where people share the same beliefs and values, there can be great collaboration from leaders of different groups. This is because they have the same cultural heritage; they speak the same language and practice the same traditions. Thus, coming together for the same purpose will enable them to make rapid decisions. For example, in the case of the community hall, everyone saw the need for the hall, and as a result, no leader hesitated. By recognising everyone's gift, value, and worth, leaders are bound to collaborate. Different leaders from different groups were schooled on the necessity of working for the same purpose of community development.

They learned to share responsibilities among themselves. For example, the women's group is organised into committees and subcommittees and headed by coordinators, Presidents, and Vice Presidents. Most of them continued to work with the notion of general interests.

No individual decisions were taken, but collective decisions were made. When Lena and her team went for the donation of benches to schools, the community leaders and even the traditional rulers were present.

The leaders of the different cooperatives work together to build trust and foster collaboration and cooperation. For example, Bongabaa Bayam-Sellam Women's Cooperative (BBSW) members can now boast of having shares in their cooperatives. These women had opened savings accounts with the Jakiri Micro Finance Institution and became members. During the general assembly of this Micro Finance Institution, the women created an impact by voting for one of them and a member's husband to be part of the management team of the Micro Finance Institution. They also came together as a strong force and elected one of their members as a parliamentarian in the National Assembly. They ensured they came together strongly to stamp out the indiscipline caused by the market boys or intermediaries in the potato market.

The leaders of the different groups of people living with disabilities from different councils came together to work with the Divisional Delegate of Social Welfare. They also came out as a strong group requesting their rights and recognition as persons living with disabilities, and the people of the social welfare office in Kumbo supported them.

The idea of the Nkumbiwa Development Forum group coming together to launch a book fair to promote reading culture and distribute books to several schools was also a show of collective leadership for the community's sake. Despite these community achievements, it was not a bed of roses.

FIVE

The Reality of the Dream

* * *

THE DARK CORRIDOR

Whenever a dream is given to us or we nurse a passion for change, we always think things would be easy. And since the dream was given to us by God, we begin to envisage the success, how it will make us important and influential in society, and how it will positively impact the lives of our friends, relatives and community at large. During this imaginative period, we never tailor our minds towards possible difficulties, challenges, or resistance from people, because all we see is validation; we see through our imaginations, people embracing only the ideas that will realise the dream.

But this is often not the reality because dreams require changing the status quo. Most people will resist change, which is why implementing change is bound to have difficulties and obstacles from different angles. While some can appreciate the ideas and the projects, others will reject and criticise at any opportunity.

People react or approach problems differently when they do occur. When some people face difficulties, they retreat from the problems because they do not know what to do. Some people believe that they can sit and things would work for them, while some are always afraid of starting something or even trying. Some people do things only when there is an advantage or motivation. Others believe they are perfect and wonderful and cannot make mistakes but would surprisingly give up at the first obstacle.

But some people are always ready to do whatever it takes to solve their problems. They will try to face the difficulties and transform their challenges into something useful. In fact, if you have never tried anything in life, you will never understand that challenges occur whenever we want to implement something new or when something dramatic happens in our lives.

Lena dived into community development without understanding or mastering what community problems were, and who the community people were. She did not understand the definition of a leader or what a leader should do, especially in times of crisis. She knew little about herself, her character, or how far she could go. She did not master the difference between community, philanthropic, and charitable works. She did not know the reality of engaging in certain activities and projects. She did not foresee the obstacles, disappointments and difficulties of any endeavour that one takes up in life. In fact, it was only when she had gone deep into the implementation of some of the projects that she recognised inevitable setbacks, which stemmed from her, from the community people themselves, from the processes and procedures of implementing some projects, and some from the community or environment. Some of these setbacks included the following points.

LACK OF SELF-CONFIDENCE AND SELF-AWARENESS

When you do not feel your worth, your good intentions can be distorted. Lena always felt unsure of herself. She believed certain things were meant for some people, and some were lucky. She considered herself someone who could not talk or speak eloquently. These ideas prevented her from practising with a law firm despite her studies in the faculty of law. She used to have this inner voice that kept on saying, "You cannot do it; it is not meant for you." "What will people say about you or about what you are doing?"

While pursuing university studies, she believed she was not a good student. She only managed to have good marks and would admire those who were actually performing well. Studies weren't easy for her, especially as a married woman. She used to feel very bad because her friends could attend all the parties in Yaounde, and she couldn't go with them. During classes, they would discuss all their pleasant experiences in the town. At that time, she felt that marital life was so frustrating; she was even wondering why she had to get married at that time, and these thoughts kept frustrating her.

When she started the Women's Group, she wanted them to look for someone to lead them. She then proposed Madame Titi, a very eloquent woman. She believed this woman was right to lead the women because of her personality. She saw some leadership qualities in this woman and did not believe she could lead the women. Madame Titi responded, "Lena, I think you can be our president. I think you stand a good chance of taking this group forward." To Lena's surprise, Madame Titi turned down her request and continued to say, "No, Lena, when someone comes up with an idea, the person should be able to execute what he or she has in mind. I believe it is your idea, so you should lead the group." It was embarrassing for Lena; she thought that Madame Titi was against the idea and was convinced she disapproved of creating the Women's Group. Lena saw some potential in someone else and not in herself. She did not believe she could lead the group but had to accept Madam Titi's proposal. She had no choice and became a leader by circumstance. That decision by Madam Titi was the beginning of Lena's leadership journey. She was always stressed out each time the meeting day approached. She would panic about what to say. However, she started organising women's meetings every second Saturday of the month at Mrs. Tekere's residence. During the first meeting, she politely requested someone to pray and chair the meeting. Lena continued harbouring this feeling and difficulty of controlling a group that was made up of many senior women with a lot more cultural and family experiences than she had.

During the fourth session, she had to work out a strategy to identify other committed women with whom to work and to convince them to become members of the team for the proper functioning of the group. At that time, she was not even convinced or sure of what she said or did, but she had to manage the women and the meetings.

Sometimes, Lena's lack of courage would make her wonder how she came into this whole issue of mobilising women and would felt like giving up. She would wonder what pushed her or who asked her to participate in such activities. She would become so frustrated if problems arose and she could not solve them. The thought that she would be held responsible and accountable for the failure of any of the events was traumatising. This also created a lot of distress because Lena was often not convinced about her entourage, what to say and how to say it.

Self-awareness is about knowing who you are. It is the ability to see yourself clearly and objectively. Knowing who you are and how others perceive you is good, without which you will create an uncomfortable environment for you and your people. You must recognise and understand your emotions, values, beliefs, behaviour, passions, and purpose. Knowing your strengths, weaknesses, temperaments, habits, and values is suitable for a leader. When you know who you are, you can create a peaceful working environment for your people, and they will build trust in you. Sometimes you may think you are doing a great job, but your team members see you differently, and they would complain behind your back.

It is good to be aware of your outside and inside feelings. What you think of yourself and tell others must match your reputation. By being open, honest, and transparent with others, you demonstrate that you have created a safe place for them and that you are ready and able to adapt to the changing and challenging situations that can befall them.

Lack of self-awareness can create a toxic environment with mistrust and conflicts with one another. You can be perceived as a bully or dictator if you are unaware of how others will view your decisions and behaviour. Lena had the attitude of always proposing ideas to the women during meetings, and some people did not appreciate that. Some members did not see why one person should always bring up ideas, and their comments were often very negative.

Lack of self-awareness tends to limit one's abilities in performance. During one of our meetings, a woman stood up and declared that they did not want authoritative meetings. "We don't want autocratic meetings, eeh!" This was because Lena brought up a proposal that this lady did not like. The lady started convincing other women with her own ideas. She claimed that as a president, Lena always enforced her own ideas and would not accept other people's ideas. These issues, which were never intentional, demoralised Lena so much that she decided never to bring up ideas to the group. Tensions started cropping up in the group. Lena was unaware of the significant consequences of group members' reactions. At that time, she was so naïve and unaware of how to go about such problems for the good functioning of the group. In fact, she did not know what to do. Some decisions she took on behalf of the group, for the good of the people, became points of disunity and caused many problems among members. She thought and believed she was doing a good job, only to realise that some members rejected her proposals. She felt like giving up the leadership.

Lack of self-awareness will lead to poor collaboration among team members, and one can end up carrying the burden alone. This can lead to the slow progress of the group. As the women's group president, she noticed the existence of parallel meetings in the different neighbourhoods after the official meetings. One lady, Miss Geana, left the group because the president was appreciated for her impactful activities. Her words, "I cannot accept that all of us should be working and only the President is being seen or promoted." According to Geana, she did not see why recognition should be given to one person, the President, or why the President should be appreciated for a job well done by a group and such stories in a women's group can only be gotten from gossip. Those were challenging moments for Lena. Such moments can block one's self-esteem because they can prevent one from initiating new ideas or setting other goals for the good of the group. As the president, Lena found that these issues have created some difficult memories to keep away.

It is easy to forgive but not easy to forget. Sometimes you think you have forgotten the issues, but when you meet the person or sit alone, those bad memories still come up. These incidents pushed Lena to conceive ideas and execute them without seeking other people's opinions. This is because she realised that some women love to have posts of responsibilities, but they cannot do what the post entails, or some women deliberately refuse to do the job. The problem in the Women's Group to this day is that the group is made up of people of the same community with the same cultural heritage, and the president has no right to expel any member because they are all linked together by their shared cultural heritage.

The most challenging part has been to learn how to work or get along with those who do not believe in the vision and connect with those who are not ready for the good functioning of the group. This is because working together with people can create an atmosphere of trust and collaboration. You need to understand how others perceive you. It is said that to be an effective leader, you must be able to lead yourself before leading others. It is also not easy to lead oneself. It is not easy to do what you say. Knowing who you are and what others think of you is difficult. We all have our blind spots. It is so hard to learn how to criticise yourself and accept criticism from others. Leading yourself cannot be easy if you do not know who you are and what you stand for.

LACK OF FUNDING

Project funding refers to the process of obtaining resources that will enable you to carry out projects. As a non-profit, the only reason to apply for funding is to create change in the community. To create this change, many people, such as community members who are beneficiaries, donors, other partners, and officials like mayors and councillors, are considered. The funding can come from these people through grants or donations. Funding community projects can be very demanding because you would not only need to identify these partners but also be able to state how much money you need and the justification for how the money will be spent. These requirements for the obtainment of funds must be fulfilled. You will need to plan, even with the help of experts, to have the funds, because the funds you request should align with the project's mission. This process became so cumbersome for Lena.

Lena needed these funds because she had identified a lot of needs in the community like the community hall in Yaounde, village schools without benches, the needs of persons with disabilities, the education of school drops-outs, upgrading of standards of education for nursery and primary school teachers, career orientation for youths, financial support to the rural women, need for women's economic empowerment centres. Lena made several attempts to search for funds from several areas, like international organisations, but she failed because she had limited knowledge of the processes and procedures for obtaining funds.

She resorted to organising fundraising events in the community. This was the only way she could get funds to solve these problems. Fundraising events are great because members of the community are concerned. They will not just give the money but participate in realising the projects. The events also attracted dedicated and talented individuals of the community who, at the same time, can amplify the project's image and promote the community's growth. Lena organised several fundraising events, like the one in April 1998 for the "purpose of purchasing a piece of land for the construction of the hall" and one for the roofing of the community dubbed "Operation two sheets of zinc." Several other fundraising events for the donation of benches to primary schools and basic necessities to persons living with disabilities in Kumbo were organised by Lena.

Lena went countless times to all the elders and important personalities of the Kumbo community in Yaounde who could donate money for these projects. She became a nuisance in the community due to her fundraising efforts. She had to stop and look for other sources of revenue, which she could not find. Some projects were not completed due to the lack of funds.

LIMITED ENGAGEMENT AND LACK OF TRUST

The unwillingness, lack of cooperation, and commitment of members of a group can create many problems in the group. When people do not trust the leader, they do not engage in whatever the leader says and does. Identifying people who believe in one's vision takes a lot of maturity.

People have different motives for joining groups. Some people join because of their interest, and when they are unsatisfied, they drop out. In the Women's Group, some women would sit in the meetings without paying attention, demonstrating a lack of enthusiasm in the meeting activities. Other members, especially the enlightened ones, usually came late for the meetings when most decisions had already been taken, and would want to reverse the decisions taken in their absence. This group of women would hardly propose anything concrete to the group but were always ready to reject and oppose what other women had agreed upon. It is not easy to manage people with negative spirits. Some members came for meetings for routine purposes and were not ready to follow up on what was being discussed in the meetings. Some women came for meetings just to socialise or relax. They never cared about what was going on during the meetings. Sometimes, important issues that were supposed to be discussed by the group during meetings were neglected, and instead, the focus was on gossip.

Some women are fond of complaining about everything. When you involve them in the activities, they are never available. When you carry out the activities without them, they complain. They do not always have the time. Sometimes, you are confused, and this ends up creating a very uncomfortable environment. Some of the members lacked discipline and commitment, which is necessary for the good functioning of the group. They do not take the time to understand the plans and objectives of the group.

Due to the cultural attachments to their beliefs, values, and habits, some men in the community do not see the importance of cultural or social meetings held by different women's groups. While some would allow their wives to attend meetings, others see meetings as a place for disorienting women and would prevent them from such gatherings. Some of them have a very negative mindset about women and their group activities. They tend to prohibit their women from attending meetings. Most men of the Muslim communities do not find any reason for allowing their wives to go to school or even join women's groups.

Most often, there is a lack of faith in women's activities. Lena realised that whenever a woman's idea or solution to a problem came up during community meetings, some men would reject it just because it came from a woman, without thinking of the impact. Such men always consider women's contribution to be minimal. They are usually very nonchalant and often shun women's ideas. Some men have the misconception that as a prominent woman of a community, one's mission is to misdirect other women. They do not want to hear or talk about concepts like gender equality, violence against women, International Women's Day, etc. In fact, Lena felt frustrated because some men believed that being a female leader was tantamount to the manipulation of women. Due to such misunderstandings and misconceptions, several skills are needed to manage the situation. Sadly, Lena had not yet acquired such skills.

COMMUNITY PEOPLE AND COMMUNITY PROBLEMS

Each community is made up of different people with different beliefs, values, and agendas. Community problems need to be well identified and analysed. Community members need to be involved in solving the problems. With Lena's dream for the community, it was not easy to implement what was planned. Lena and her team identified most of the problems and started tackling them. They did not take the time to brainstorm or understand some of the issues and the mindset of the people concerned.

Jumping to fix problems without the community's input can bring more problems. That is why Lena had issues with some people not showing interest and not contributing to raising the funds, disengaging from the work, and searching for their own interests. Lena realised that not everyone was interested in charitable or philanthropic work. In this community, some people prefer to use their money in the palaces to gain titles rather than engage in community work. Such people do not care, would not even appreciate what others are doing, and would be happy if that money were given to them.

Some people delight in misjudging others; consequently, their actions would create pain for others. There was a time Lena tried to work with people of the Kumbo community in the Diaspora to raise funds for a project to provide benches to schools in Kumbo. Funds were actually raised for the project because most people concerned contributed. But before we could even commence the project, some of them raised a negative alarm that Lena had swindled the money. There was a lack of trust, which was so frustrating and embarrassing. From that day, Lena vowed never to seek funds or support from any member of the Kumbo community in the Diaspora.

ABSENCE OF ROLE MODELS AND MENTORS

A role model is someone who sets an example that others can emulate. A mentor is someone who can help others through life's difficulties. People naturally look up to role models because they can inspire others through their character and behaviour. Because they are role models, they can influence others with their actions. If a role model can show strong qualities like integrity, honesty, and openness, she will encourage others to behave in a similar way.

Lena had many people who could criticise negatively, but no one to guide her. Most people around her were not used to sharing stories that could help others. She depended so much on herself. Several times, she made mistakes, realised and corrected them by herself. It can be frustrating to see someone who can help but would rather watch you make mistakes. We live in an environment where most people do not want to take the responsibility of pointing out the errors, omissions, and misdeeds of others for fear of eventual problems. Lena grew up in this environment where people do not want to confront reality.

DIFFICULTIES IN BUILDING A TEAM

In this environment, it was not easy for Lena to identify other women who were ready to sacrifice to help others through their difficulties. Because of circumstances, Lena became a "do-it-all-by-yourself" person. Identifying potential women who were ready to accept leadership roles was challenging. Many women are not ready to align with the group's goals and objectives because they do not understand what leadership entails or why they should become leaders. So, it became difficult to build a strong and effective team.

A good team is made up of people who are more understanding because they are aware of the consequences of their actions. They can improve decision-making. They are aware of their emotions and biases when making decisions, especially where their choices have a significant impact. They know themselves and are open and ready to receive feedback from their actions. They are prepared to change and work for the needs of the people they lead. They know their limitations and can modify their mindsets. They can keep their emotions in check to prevent conflicts. They are authentic, trustworthy, and credible because they are ready to recognise their own mistakes and limitations.

Identifying such women in the Women's Group was challenging, given that Lena mainly worked with grassroots women.

It is also a challenge to put in the time and energy to train and develop a leader or an individual, and the person quits the group after acquiring all the skills. This is very discouraging, and these are the kinds of situations that sometimes force someone to continue working alone. Lena was the Women's Group president for over fifteen years, not because she wanted to, but because no one was ready and willing to take up the responsibility. Women with less educational backgrounds were those loyal and prepared to take up leadership roles. So, it became so difficult to have annual reports of activities or historical records for future reference.

It was not easy to build a good team that could eventually act as mentors to other young people. The most significant problem was that the members of these groups were of the same cultural heritage, people from the community, and sometimes, one just had to succumb to their whims and caprices.

DIFFICULTIES IN ASSESSING THE IMPACT OF CHANGE

Data collection, data analysis, writing, and reporting findings must be done to measure and evaluate change. Several changes occurred in this community from the initial projects, but the most challenging part was measuring and evaluating what had changed. There were no experts to write and report all those changes. There was no one to document all that was being done. Everything was carried out with local people who could only tell stories. There was no proper planning with action plans for the implementation of projects, which made it challenging to apply the traditional way of monitoring and evaluating a project.

Lena and her team relied on observations of the different changes in the community. They resorted to listening to conversations from people to hear what had actually changed in the community. Only the very people who felt the change gave testimonies of what had happened. They could also get feedback from people like mayors and councillors on the changes they had observed within the environment. What they actually did was watch people's attitudes towards change.

The verbal explanations by persons living with disabilities about their new lives, the *bayam-sellam* women about the changes in their sales and farm yields, and the young boys who could testify to the changes they had experienced in their lives encouraged Lena and her team to understand that several things had occurred. Lena would travel from Yaounde to Kumbo every October to talk with women and get their feedback on what they did, which was so demanding for her and a great challenge.

LACK OF ACCESS TO INFORMATION

There was a lack of adequate structures for accessing information, especially from public institutions. It was always difficult for the villages to approach the government institutions for information. For example, the government created a social welfare centre in Kumbo. Still, because of the lack of awareness and circulation of information from the social welfare services, those with disabilities were not making use of this centre. Parents did not see the necessity of searching for educational news or information about their children's education, so most of them remained ignorant about the services provided by the government educational centres.

Information is essential to our daily lives and is needed in every domain. Information is important because we need information for learning, education, and health and wellness purposes. In this community, most people only got information about certain happenings in and out of the community from the churches. It became challenging to gather information for any project implementation. There was just one community library in Kumbo, which was a gift from an elder, and most people were not interested in frequenting this library because of a lack of awareness of the importance of a library.

Most people were not sensitised on their health issues. Women had to trek long distances to the hospital to get information about their health situations. Most information about children's vaccinations was not elaborately carried out, and most people from the hinterlands remained ignorant about vaccines.

Despite these challenges, Lena did not give up. She cannot tell what kept her going, but she had to adopt certain strategies to keep moving. Lena realised she had gone so deep into community activities that there was no turning back. She had to reflect and evaluate herself and her actions to understand if she was on the right track.

The reality is that whatever your dream in life is, the journey to achieving it will be cumbersome and never easy. You will always encounter several setbacks, obstacles, and difficulties. It was also essential to know why there were many challenges and the root causes of these difficulties.

SIX

The Core of the Challenges

* * *

If you cannot identify a problem, you won't be able to solve it. If you do not understand or master your problem, you cannot have the correct answer. You must look for the root causes of your problems, without which you will not create the impact. The following factors have been the root causes of the challenges.

A LACK OF VISION OR SENSE OF DIRECTION

In 1996, when Lena started working with the first women's group, she had no knowledge of the word 'vision'. She came up with the idea of creating a women's group to build and promote unity, solidarity, and development amongst women. This idea started growing, but she did not really master herself or how groups function. When she had this idea, she did not know the direction in which she was taking the group. She only saw the importance of people coming together, but she did not master the depths of such a gathering, and her only reason for the group's existence was that they were strangers in the land of Yaounde.

The group members did not master the full meaning of

the idea. There were no written plans on how the group would develop, get resources, or be managed. There were no set goals and objectives outlined for the group. Everything was done by trial and error. The members thought of coming together to meet one another, but they did not really believe or have confidence in themselves. The women did not master the purpose of the creation of the group. To them, it was a regular gathering of women of a particular community residing outside their villages.

Problems started creeping into this group from 2008, resulting in the disengagement of some members. In 2009, when Lena read John Maxwell's book, *Leadership Promises for Your Week*, she was inspired by this quote: "Where there is no vision, the people perish." Henceforth, Lena learned that a group could have plenty of talents, resources and opportunities, but without a vision, the group will not progress. She started questioning, examining herself, and her purpose of creating the group.

Without a clear vision of what a leader wants to do, the leader will have problems. The vision must come first before the achievements. The vision must be clearly communicated to all the members of the group. The group members did not understand what community development was all about. The group started solving community problems without mastering the landscape of the problems.

In fact, you must master what you are doing and why you are doing it before searching for ways to achieve results. The leader's vision is critical because it is often said that the leader is the one who sees the way and must show the path to others, without which the people will get off course. The members joined the group with no aims and plans for themselves and the future.

WEAKNESSES, MISTAKES, AND OMISSIONS

Whenever Lena was criticised or challenged, she always felt disappointed and frustrated. She would desist from making important decisions and actions that could impact the group, often retreating from the issues. Lena felt very unhappy when she was criticised for being autocratic and authoritative.

In 1978, during the first year of Lena's university studies, there was a student strike on the university campus, where students wanted to demonstrate their anger and dissatisfaction with the administration of the Law Faculty. In fact, she did not know why there was a student strike on campus, and she had never been curious about finding out why students were disgruntled. To avoid problems, she stayed at home. When her husband asked her the reason for the students' strike, she could not explain. He was embarrassed and cautioned her that, as a student, she was supposed to know why there was a strike in her school. Lena felt bad because she was a first-year student and had not mastered the older students' activities. She felt belittled and angry.

She remembers one day she wanted to take a taxi from the Obili neighbourhood to the Ministry of Public Service, known in the French language as *Ministère de la Fonction Publique*. She stopped a taxi and pronounced the word "Function Public" in English, and everybody in the car screamed with laughter. The driver did not pick her up because everyone laughed. She knew something was wrong but could not identify what was wrong. She stood there, frustrated and afraid of taking the next taxi. She felt bad about herself.

She made several mistakes, like not planning and setting goals for the group. Each time an idea came to her, she would just start executing without actually looking for the resources to carry out the project, without knowing or mastering the people who would carry out the project. This way of managing her activities drained her resources, for which she paid the price. She was the person who put in the resources needed on several occasions. She carried out projects without the right goals and objectives, only to realise her difficulties later. She had no knowledge about project management.

She also feared discussing her ideas with negative people who saw nothing good about her intentions. This also created a lot of frustration because of the many negative people we have in our communities. Convincing people who do not see anything good in someone requires a lot of effort, and it is not easy to make progress with such people around. So, Lena's best solution was to stay away from them. But can staying away from your critics solve your problem?

Listening to people is essential, and more importantly, listening to the right people. Lena did not understand that listening to others could also enable her to learn from them. She has a weakness of always talking without first listening. She is fond of dishing out her own ideas and opinions before listening to those of others. It becomes so painful when you realise your fault of not listening to others first. As the Women's Group president, she used to inadvertently interrupt someone who had the floor to speak. When she thought the point someone was raising was not suitable, or that the point had already been made by another person, she would immediately jump and interrupt the person who was yet to conclude. She would not spend much time focusing on and understanding what the person wanted to say. She was fond of always talking more than listening.

She also had the weakness of being deaf to some complaints,

considering them unimportant, and disrupting the group's proper functioning.

Again, she constantly blamed others instead of concentrating on their strengths. She believed other people were not helping her achieve her desired results. She felt alone in the game and unsupported by a particular class of women. The lack of understanding of her personality, weaknesses, and mistakes negatively affected the group atmosphere.

LACK OF BASIC SKILLS

Lena had not acquired any skills in managing people, projects, finances, and crises. And this consequently brought a lot of problems to the Women's Group. When Lena and her team started this group, everything was done verbally, and no records were kept. They usually had physical meetings and direct or face-to-face communication with members during the meetings. They could only send verbal communiques to others after the meetings in case of any emergency. Lena realised that during those meetings, what was said during one meeting ended up being explained differently by other members at different levels. There were a lot of inconsistencies. What was said during meetings had to be repeated at the next meeting for clear understanding. The person taking down minutes of the day or records was never trained. No good financial records were kept. Members kept the financial statistics or records in their memories for the next meeting. There were no cell phones at that time. Giving feedback on activities was not easy because the women had no skills in that domain. Lena had never learnt how to manage groups. They would simply imagine what to do during the meetings.

Some of the meetings were very long and unproductive.

"Meetings should be an opportunity for everyone to get to know each other and talk about the interests they have in common," says Milo O. Frank

In the case of projects, there was no proper planning and preparation. Lena did not know how to prepare, execute, monitor and control projects. For example, she wanted to help the rural women diversify their farm products, so she came up with the idea of cultivating onions by Bongabaa Bayam-Sellam Women. She met with the Secretary of State at the Ministry of Agriculture and requested her support. She asked her to bring a project plan for the onions project so that the Ministry of Agriculture could support. Lena did not know how to write a project. She went to someone to help write out a project, and this person requested the sum of five hundred thousand francs as payment for writing the project. Lena could not raise the amount of money requested, but with the help of the community elite, she raised the sum of three hundred thousand francs. Instead of paying someone to write the project, she distributed five thousand francs per group to forty-six women's groups in Jakiri and Kumbo to purchase onion seeds, eventually leading to the cultivation of onions in the community. One year later, when she visited these women, she received verbal reports of how many onion farms they had cultivated and how much was sold and consumed. She saw the impact of a "five thousand francs CFA" donation on the lives of several women. However, she could not effectively control this project because she had no mastery of evaluating and monitoring projects. But she observed that the project had had a significant impact as it changed many lives. Despite the crisis in this area, some women are still cultivating and selling onions for a living.

Concerning the construction of the Community Hall in

Yaounde, most of the financial contributors were civil servants. The project was bound to stop for some time because some community members who volunteered to supervise the job were transferred out of Yaounde. She realised that some people just wanted to be involved in the project just because they were interested in the money. Traditionally, only men construct houses in this community, and women are never involved. Even though the women raised the money for the project, they could not follow up on the effective use of the funds for the project. The project had to be suspended for months in order for financial issues to be sorted out.

With the control of finances, there was no follow-up on managing finances in the women's groups. The financial facet of every group or organisation is very delicate and should be handled meticulously. When there is a lack of transparency in the management of finances, problems are bound to occur. For example, in 1998, Lena proposed a financial scheme for the women's group. The members accepted, and a thrift and loan scheme was created. The scheme aimed to assist women in carrying out their business activities with less financial stress. Because of the lack of financial management skills, the rightful beneficiaries of the scheme never enjoyed their rights, and non-members became the beneficiaries. As president of the group, Lena was supposed to monitor and follow up on this scheme, but she did not put in the effort needed to follow up because at that time, she had not mastered the financial rules of such a structure. Consequently, the group went through a severe financial crisis due to the lack of financial management skills of all the persons in charge of the scheme.

When managing crises and conflicts, one must be tactful. For example, elections became a source of conflict and misunderstanding among the women's group members in Yaounde. During the election of executive leaders, the most qualified women did not present their candidacies due to a lack of self-confidence. Some women believed that being a leader was very demanding, so they could not present their candidacies for fear of undertaking the tedious tasks that such a post of responsibility entails. In 2005, as the group's founder and with no one ready to lead, Lena was obliged to present herself to carry the group forward. No other candidate came up. She was the lone candidate, and after the elections, many negative members came up to criticise and incite others to create disorder. At the end of the elections, significant criticisms came from the same people who refused to vie for the different posts of responsibility available for the elections.

In 2015, Lena came up with the idea that some members of the women's group be trained to manage the group eventually. She had served for a long time as president and did not want to continue in that capacity. No woman was willing to take over. Lena identified ten women who could be trained to handle the group. From these ten women, the members had to elect the best three women to manage the group for five years, and the best three women were identified. This event brought back leadership squabbles and a lot of disorder, hatred, and disunity to the community, as it was led by those who thought they were qualified but were not elected. This also had consequences for the people of the Kumbo community in Yaounde. And much effort was needed to bring peace and unity back to the group and the community.

LACK OF PROPER COMMUNICATION STRATEGIES

Communication strategies are plans for conveying messages concerning events and situations to your audience. A group should always have a plan for creating awareness, building interests, and informing people about what is happening in the group. If you do not know how to communicate or channel your message to the people, they will not grasp what you want to do. When people do not master what is happening, there is room for gossip and different interpretations. When people understand what they are doing, they perform excellently and creatively.

Lena grew up timid and was not used to talking too much. She always preferred reading over talking. Talking in public or knowing what to say had always been a problem for her. She grew up in an environment where young girls could not express themselves. You were to be seen and not heard. She was never open to debates, discussions, or open conversations with elders or friends. Her inability to communicate the clear goals and objectives of the group to the members was another factor that created many problems. When she started her community work, she realised her inability to express herself and her ideas to people. She was fond of always asking others to explain what she was doing. She later realised that when someone is asked to talk on another's behalf, the right message is never conveyed to the listeners. When it came to talking to journalists about her ideas, it was never very easy for her, as public speaking has never been her forte. Whenever a microphone was given to her to talk, everything would disappear from her mind. She would not know what to say. She saw her limits in communicating her ideas. It took her a long time to have the courage to talk and grant interviews about her works. She realised she had done so much without communicating what she was doing to other stakeholders. Many people were not aware of her works. Moreover, she did not see the reason for people to know what she was doing. She believed the work would speak for itself, so she had no objective in granting interviews about her work. She constantly felt and believed that she was not a good speaker.

When a message is not well communicated to the people, it can create a lot of misunderstandings and misjudgments. Many people were unaware of the vision, and some are known for criticising everything from face value. Lena's inability to communicate her ideas stemmed from her primary school days, where the culture of reading books and communicating was not a priority. She was not open to much talking.

POOR STRUCTURING OF THE GROUPS

Some problems in the women's group came up because the group was not well organised. In a good structure, members would understand their different roles. They would be given tasks and roles to play. They are expected to perform their various roles in a committed way. Most members became registered members just because of their cultural identity. They never cared about doing anything because their only reason for being in the group was the language that bound them. The roles were poorly identified, so the members never understood them. In a group where members do not know what is expected of them, there are bound to be problems. Many women became members just because of cultural solidarity and not because of the contributions that they had to bring to the group. There were no laid-down rules and regulations for discipline. For example, with the women's group, Lena had not mastered the functioning of groups. She did not really know how to manage members within groups. She had no idea about group dynamics and only learnt about it in 2022.

INADEQUATE COMPETENCIES OF THE GRASSROOTS WOMEN

Women, generally from their different cultural and traditional backgrounds, have barriers that prevent them from progressing, especially women in rural communities. Lena worked with two groups of women with varying styles of living: rural women and urban low-income women. The rural women are mostly subsistent farmers and petty traders. The urban low-income women, like those in the women's group, were women who found themselves in the cities as housewives, home managers, babysitters, and small business owners.

They are mostly women who dropped out of school for one reason or another, with a low standard of education and dependency rate; most of them lacked the will and determination to go back to school. As the rural women continued farming, those in the cities were initiated and encouraged to carry out petty trading in the cities to sustain their lives. Even though they were so loyal to the group, it wasn't easy to have women in these groups who could manage the group and give adequate reports of their activities for the group's progress.

INABILITY TO ANALYSE COMMUNITY PROBLEMS

Analysing the problem involves thinking carefully about the issue before the solution. When you carefully analyse a project, it will enable you to understand the people's feelings about the project. It will determine whether the people like the project or not. Since the project is for the people, their support will make it sustainable. If we take the time to understand the project carefully, it will help us to carry out the work. This was not the case with the projects Lena and her team implemented. They did not take the time to analyse some of the community's problems. In the case of the identified projects, Lena and her team initiated the projects for the people. They felt that the people needed what they offered. In that case, the projects were taken to the people and were not identified by the people themselves. In the case of planting trees, the people of the community did not know why Lena and her team were planting trees. It was the Ministry of Environment that sponsored the project because it was the mission of that ministry to encourage communities to plant trees to prevent soil degradation and climate change. Still, the concepts were not well explained to the population.

Carefully analysing the problem will help you to understand the people or the stakeholders involved in the project. In the case of the hall construction, the right people to carry out the work were not identified. The people who carried out the project were civil servants who volunteered to do the job for the love of their community, not because they were experts. That is why the project encountered a lot of difficulties and took a longer period to be completed than was expected.

Carefully analysing the problem will help you to understand its root causes. Once the root causes are understood, you can solve the problem and establish systems and policies that will prevent the problem from recurring. If people can take the time to reflect on the issues or problems, they will be able to understand if the problem can be solved. They will understand how the problem will affect people. They will know if the problems are caused by individuals, by nature or environment, or by the cultural beliefs and values of the community members. They will be able to identify the people or agents in the community who will change the situation, and there will be community engagement.

Carefully analysing the problems can help you to understand the resources needed for the project. A better understanding of the problem will help you know how much is required for the project's success. You would look for the contribution of the people to the project to make them understand that the project is for them. There were no planned budgets for most of the projects Lena and her team carried out. They could not identify the sources of income for the projects. Sometimes, she was caught up in the situation, and as the initiator of most of the projects, she was the person who put in the resources needed on several occasions.

Lena and her team did not take the time to find out the root causes of the problems, the stakeholders and the resources. Most projects were carried out without the right goals and objectives, only to discover the mistakes and failures later. If people can carefully understand a project before engaging with the implementation, it would help them identify the risks involved in the project. Some of the projects were abandoned due to a lack of resources and no committed leaders to carry on the projects.

SEVEN

Overcoming the Challenges

* * *

Challenges are difficulties in our lives, but they are also good and vital parts of life. No human venture can be successful without setbacks. You will not understand the difficulties in anything if you have not tried it. Whenever one starts anything, obstacles may slow or stop one from achieving what one intended. These obstacles can sometimes be of our own making, imposed by others, or even inherent to the environment in which we find ourselves.

Sometimes one must go through difficult situations or circumstances to learn. If you have never faced challenging moments, you will never understand what you are capable of and what you are truly made of. In the dark corridor, Lena had anger, pain, confusion, and misunderstandings with people from different mindsets and cultures. To emerge from the dark corridor was not an easy task. Changing one's mind and habits is not a piece of cake. Lena needed some time to figure out who she was before deciding what she wanted to do. She then decided to strengthen her character and vision, develop her competencies and build a strong attitude. These actions helped her gain deeper insights into her purpose, personality, values, and actions, and enabled her to move forward on her journey.

UNDERSTANDING HER STRENGTHS AND IDENTITY
Her personality

A leader's character is essential. When we discuss character, we refer to the strengths and choices of a leader. A leader can choose to be either a good or a bad leader. A leader can choose to develop a positive or negative character, depending on their personality traits. He or she can choose to be wicked or kind. How a leader deals with the circumstances of life tells you many things about his or her character and personality. A leader with a negative mindset cannot be trusted. People follow leaders who are well-behaved. No one likes to work with an unreliable or untrustworthy person.

After coming a long way, Lena now understands the kind of person she is, what she can and cannot do, and what she stands for. She decided to build a positive mindset that enabled her to achieve more. She continued to work with determination to succeed in whatever she did. Understanding her traits as a perfectionist and a joyful person who wants things to be done with attention to detail, she is always anxious about not failing. She is a person of action and results. Whenever Lena and her team organise events, she always ensures everything is well organised. She just discovered that God has given her several talents and many qualities of a leader. She believes she has been unable to develop some of her hidden talents. She has been endowed with so much, and with gratitude, she tries to share with others. Ensuring that she is honest and transparent in everything she does has earned her the trust of several women, who remain loyal to her vision to this day.

Naturally, she is humble, but having led and navigated through challenges, mistakes, and failures, she has developed a distinct character. She used to shy away from issues, complicated and hurting issues, but now she tends to face those issues with confidence. As Jayne Leonard Beaton puts it, "If you fear your struggles, your struggles will consume you, but if you face your struggles, you will overcome them." She learned valuable lessons from every obstacle she encountered. When you are a person of integrity, many people will listen to you, confide in you, and respect you.

She also discovered her quick-to-forgive character, although she finds it hard to forget the incidents. Your character inspires trust, and you become a person of influence.

Her attitude

Her resilient, daring, and never-give-up attitude has been her strength.

While working with women, Lena took some decisive decisions and actions that saved the group from collapsing because of her "never-give-up" attitude. She discovered that when faced with difficulties or challenges, she becomes stronger. She tends to work harder when she is criticised. She always wants to show her critics that she is right. The financial and leadership crisis in the women's group made her discover some of her potential. In times of crisis, one needs to be flexible in taking suitable or adaptable decisions that will solve the problems.

This daring attitude has been a part of her since her youth. She would always go beyond the expected, which is how she discovered herself and some of her abilities. She would manage everything at home, carrying out tasks without complaining. Her parents used to send her to do their errands very early in the mornings, and back then, there were no township taxis, no telephones, and no bike riders. Sometimes she would be whisked out of bed as early as five in the morning to deliver a message in another village many kilometres away. Before her mother could return from the farm, she had prepared the evening meal. She recalls that she began splitting wood at a very young age. While in high school, she studied economics, a subject she had not pursued in secondary school. After studying English law at the University of Yaounde, she privately pursued studies in administrative public law. This took her to the School of Administration and Magistracy, where she graduated as a tax inspector.

As a leader, it is good to build a resilient attitude. You must learn to work under pressure, as it is also a valuable learning experience. Lena realised her ability to organise events, to withstand difficult circumstances, and to go the extra mile to do whatever it takes. You must learn to be tough during tough times; if not, your goals will not be met. It is always good to bounce back. This requires a great deal of patience and perseverance. You must be determined to look back at where you started and decide to continue. When you find yourself in difficulties, you have to take time to reflect and figure out what to do. Always accept the challenges and then look for solutions. As a leader, one must be flexible and ready to adapt to changes. The pain of working and managing difficulties has been a good lesson and inspiration for Lena.

Your attitude should serve as an inspiration to your followers. Even when things look bleak and followers are disheartened, the leader must stay positive, maintain a sense of optimism and hope to face the challenges. Additionally, cultivating a spirit of gratitude is crucial for a leader. No one can succeed alone; you must show appreciation to those who have helped you throughout your life. That is why, at the end of each year, in our different groups, Lena and her team try to show appreciation to some hard-working members by awarding prizes to them. Your attitude should inspire others to follow in your footsteps.

Her Creativity

Creating strategies for managing people has become an essential issue on Lena's agenda. She learned that leadership is about taking key actions. It is about putting your good ideas into concrete action. A good leader should be creative. Only a leader with a good, creative spirit can initiate actions that will impact others. A leader must bring out those ideas that will change the community and the lives of those within it. Let your actions demonstrate that you are committed to helping people and adding value to them, and they will trust you and collaborate with you. A leader's actions should be for the service of the people. This would enable the people to trust the leader. So, Lena learned to consistently implement those ideas that will impact people's lives and influence others.

Lena's creative spirit is inborn, so she strengthened this aspect. In most of her groups, she is always the first person to come up with ideas for the groups to implement, and this enabled her to create several structures like the thrift and loan scheme, which has become a financial cooperative known as the Women's Trust Fund, the Women's Savings Schemes, the Food Cooperatives, Self-Help Groups, Wellness Programs, Farmers'

Input schemes, Poverty schemes. These structures have changed the lives of many grassroots men and women in this leadership journey.

Her Passion

When you love your work, you approach it with energy, excellence, and a clear focus on your goals and objectives. Lena finally realised that her life has been about nurturing and motivating people, especially women and young girls. She has been so passionate about women having better lives.

Her way of constantly talking with women led to discovering her purpose. She discovered her persistent and sociable nature as she mingled with the women. She likes advising and educating people, especially women and young girls. She always shows keen interest when women talk about their challenges. She loves encouraging people, especially young people, to use their talents. She feels happy and satisfied after discussing and sharing stories with young girls. When she is in the village, she always shares her stories with others. Sharing her stories and experiences has been one way of changing the mindsets of young girls in her network.

DEVELOPING "THE OTHER PERSON'S" MINDSET

Lena learned to see things from other people's perspectives. She began to consider the broader perspective. Working with grassroots women, she learned to believe in and understand them, to look at things from their perspective. She also realised that each person is unique and that, as a leader, you should focus on people's strengths rather than capitalising on their weaknesses. She gained the courage to turn the pages and pursue a new way of working with people because leadership is all about people.

Our environments have grown so much that people do not have faith in others. Failing to appreciate our differences and similarities has caused a lack of understanding among friends and families. Some people lack confidence in themselves and rely on others for support. When we learn to be patient and tolerant with others, we tend to build a peaceful atmosphere for everyone. To work effectively with others, you need to have confidence in them. When you cultivate a positive attitude towards others, you can have a profoundly positive impact on their lives.

When you practice the golden rule of treating others with respect and value, everything falls into place. You must be a source of encouragement to your teammates. A leader's motives for taking action should be genuine and sincere, without which you will lose the people. You must demonstrate to the people that your actions are in their best interest, not yours. The agenda should be the people's agenda, not yours. When people understand that you stand for the truth and are not out to manipulate or take advantage of them, they will build trust in you. By motivating leaders, Lena learned to implement ideas that consistently impact people's lives.

Learn to listen to others and show love and respect. Lena learned to value people, and she genuinely cares about them. Lena discovered her natural qualities of sharing and giving to others. This has enabled her to support numerous ventures led by women and individuals with disabilities within this community. She has many young people looking up to her for guidance and support in their lives. As the saying goes, "to whom much is given, much is expected." This philosophy kept her vision going.

She has realised that this feeling and love for the people brought her into community work. She spent a lot of time, energy, and money taking care of other people's problems, and that is how she came to build the association of persons living with disabilities.

ENHANCING HER SKILLS

First, Lena had to identify, master, and accept her weaknesses. Through her self-reflection and self-evaluation, she had to identify the areas where she was lacking and determine how to evolve from there. She learned that to lead better, one must know how to grow oneself. She realised that good leaders are good learners. As a leader, one must set aside energy and resources to empower oneself; therefore, she embarked on a journey of self-improvement. It all started from the Ministry of Finance, Department of Taxation, when a management program known as Management by Objectives (MBO) was introduced in 2013. Lena and other colleagues had several in-service trainings where they were trained on how to manage administrative files using information and technology programs. She learned how to manage taxpayers, tax agents, office equipment and materials, documents, and collect taxes for the state treasury. This way of working inspired Lena to consistently strive for good results, wherever she found herself. From then on, this idea became her mantra for managing her numerous activities.

Lena grew up in an environment where people had no incentive to read, so children did not develop a reading culture and lacked motivation to read. Because that was Lena's childhood environment, she never grew up with the love and culture of reading. After reading a few books she bought while visiting the United States for the first time, she realised that there was gold in the books. When she read *Miracles Happen* by Mary Kay Ash, she was inspired to create her own enterprise, which enabled her to develop and strengthen her entrepreneurial spirit. With Mary Kay's principles, Lena carved out her own philosophy: "Create something—Own something." This philosophy emphasises that everything should be done with excellence. With this philosophy, many women have established various business structures that continue to function today.

From John Maxwell's book, *Leadership Promises for the Week*, Lena understood the importance of having a vision in life. As a leader, you must lead yourself first before leading others. John Maxwell's principles helped Lena to reshape her ideas and strengthen her leadership skills. She developed a culture of continuous learning and gained a wealth of knowledge in personal skills, including communication, problem-solving, collaboration, motivation, creativity, and innovation.

Lena went for training at the Pan African Institute (PAIDWA) in Yaounde for a short course in project management. She used to conduct her activities in a hazardous manner and was convinced that taking this course would enhance her management skills. Each time she identified a problem, she would look for solutions without taking time to analyse the implications and the depths of the problem. While at PAIDWA, she learned how to prepare, plan, execute, monitor, and evaluate a project, as well as teamwork, time management, organisation, and community mobilisation. From her studies in PAIDWA, she began to believe in herself and the impact she was having on women. She understood the impact of her community activities and what it meant to "empower women." This motivated her to continue working with women. She learned how to track the records of her activities and the importance of writing and maintaining accurate reports. She also realised the importance of giving feedback after events, as it serves as encouragement for future planning.

From 2020, she enrolled in online certification classes on leadership development with John Maxwell, project management with the PMO-Global Alliance, and entrepreneurship with Coursera. After completing these trainings, she obtained certifications as a certified leadership coach, speaker, and trainer from the John Maxwell Team and as a Project Management Certified Practitioner from the PMO Global Alliance. She is currently a member of the Project Management Institute.

By listening to the ideas of others through tapes, featuring Myles Munroe, Les Brown, Jim Rohn, Jack Ma, Simon Sinek, and Jim Kwik, as well as Oprah Winfrey, Mrs. Obama, Priyanka Chopra, and Dr. Grace Lee, among others, she gained knowledge that changed her way of thinking and acting.

CHANGE OF MANAGEMENT STYLES

Through managing meetings, Lena learned to apply the knowledge she had gained from the Pan African Institute (PAIDWA). She began applying the knowledge and skills she had learned, particularly in the areas of management and communication, and the results were better-organised meetings. She conducted follow-up sessions to ensure that the scheduled meeting hours were respected. She purchased record books and ensured that all meeting decisions were documented. She made women understand the purpose of coming together to empower themselves, exchange ideas, and collaborate to promote peace. She taught women that meetings were not a place for gossip and negative competition. She made women understand that networking or sharing ideas would enable them to expand their activities.

In managing finances, she restructured the finance committees and established a follow-up committee. Members of the finance committee were then trained to be transparent and accountable in their financial activities. This committee properly managed all financial records. Lena and her team sought an expert for guidance on writing their annual financial reports.

Lena was able to create a structure for project management. A project management committee was established to identify projects for the year and provide plans for how the projects would be executed, controlled, and evaluated transparently. For new projects, the project management committee learned to work with all stakeholders, especially the direct beneficiaries of the project, to get their different opinions.

A structure for settling conflicts was created through conflict management. In the women's group, some elderly women and titleholders were elected as committee members. The committee members underwent training on how to prevent conflict. This same committee is responsible for educating members on the importance of peace and harmony in their homes.

To overcome her lapses in communication, Lena created committees and subcommittees to facilitate communication among members. She adopted the method of carefully explaining the purpose and objectives of every activity to the group. She also learned to listen to others before making decisions because seeking other people's opinions is also essential. With the rapid advancement in technology and social media, communication has become easier for groups. Lena and her team took the courage to learn how to give good reports for their activities. She decided to train herself to speak and communicate better.

IMPLEMENTATION OF SOME LEADERSHIP TECHNIQUES

Applying new leadership styles

When Lena understood the importance of the Internet, she started spending quality time on it, learning about leadership. With knowledge of people, their personality traits, and how groups function, she could discern the leadership styles that suited her vision, as they can create significant impact in people's lives. Understanding and mastering the various leadership styles and knowing how to apply them gave Lena the confidence to continue working with women. She learned and understood always to apply the why, the what, the when, and the how mindset when carrying out her activities. She learned that different leadership styles can be used at any time, depending on the circumstances in which a leader finds themselves. Sometimes, when the rules and regulations are not respected and the going is tough, a leader can hit the table and stay firm in his/her decisions as well. Circumstances can make a leader hard on people, but they can still use a soft approach to solve the same problem or negotiate issues with them. From Lena's experiences and purpose, the environment, and her target group of people, she embarked on three leadership styles: the transformational leadership style, the servant leadership style, and the pace-setting leadership style.

Delegation of Roles to Group Members

These leadership styles helped Lena develop herself and others as she learned to always assign group roles or duties to team members to ensure the group's good functioning.

Group roles are duties assigned to members to carry out tasks to build or manage the group. Group roles help people stay focused and work together, significantly contributing to the group's success and helping them feel like part of it. Leaders of the group have the roles of leading, facilitating, coaching, and giving advice to other group members.

Some other leaders have the role of ensuring that everyone understands the group's vision, goals, and objectives. They carry out group meetings, and they are the ones to encourage others to come up with ideas. Other group members are responsible for contributing ideas, monitoring, and following up on the group's activities. Some will arbitrate in times of conflict and ensure peace and harmony in the group. In this group, we also have people who take down reports and feedback on all the group's happenings. Some will criticise and put the group on the right track. Having these roles requires significant commitment from all the members.

The Women's Group has a membership of two hundred and fifty persons. The group has fifteen branches divided into three zones, and their activities are managed through five committees: the economic, social, cultural, project and advisory committees. Four general presidents oversee these committees and the zones, while branch presidents manage the members within their respective branches. These different roles have been assigned to these leaders, who have been well-trained to manage them.

It is not advisable to be a "do-it-all-by-yourself" leader. Sometimes we feel that if you allow others to do it, things will collapse. When we delegate tasks, we share the responsibilities. It can improve the performance and productivity of members. If you allow others to do the work, they will learn to be creative and acquire problem-solving skills. The workload will be reduced, as many people will be given the opportunity to do the work. If you can find team members who can perform tasks almost as well as you can, then you can delegate some tasks to them, but hold them accountable. This will create a conducive environment for trust, as members will also feel motivated to complete the work. It's a good idea to encourage others' contributions.

In the Women's Group, Lena and her team identified leaders who were able and willing to work, demonstrating consistency and commitment in their daily activities. At the beginning of the year, they are assigned different tasks, and the follow-up team is responsible for ensuring that these tasks are well-coordinated.

Lena had to identify some members of the group who were always there for the effective functioning of the group. Nobody does anything alone, so identifying people around you who can buy into your vision is crucial. This is necessary because each person brings unique skills to the team, and no one wins unless everyone on the team gives their best. It is said that success does not only come from what you know but also from who you know.

If you are alone, you are not leading anyone. As Mother Teresa says, "You can do what I cannot do. I can do what you cannot do. Together, we can do great things." However, the people you want to bring around must be those who will add value—individuals with excellence, maturity, and good character. John Maxwell says that a leader's potential is determined by those closest to him/her. You must prepare people to carry on your vision, objectives, values, and philosophy. When you bring in people with strengths in your area of weakness, they will complement what you cannot do, thereby increasing the group's overall performance. As a leader, the only solution is to train and empower those who are ready and willing to perform.

DEVELOPING THE COMPETENCES OF GRASSROOTS WOMEN

When given the right opportunities, grassroots women can become effective change agents in their community. Most of them have low self-esteem and a lack of self-confidence due to their environment, which can lead to poor performance.

Through adult literacy classes, women continued to learn and improve their reading and writing skills. Some women in Yaounde returned to evening school to reacquire their knowledge. Several workshops were organised to train women in creating and managing their businesses, promoting financial literacy, and acquiring digital skills. For example, during the COVID-19 pandemic, many women were able to buy and sell their products online and send and receive money through the mobile money systems that the state had implemented.

Lena and her team also trained women through workshops and seminars to build their capacity to manage their health issues through the wellness program. Educational talks during meetings on self-care and home management have boosted women's abilities. As a result of these efforts, women gained economic empowerment. They gained knowledge in leadership, entrepreneurship, financial literacy, Digital literacy, Personnel development, and management.

INVOLVEMENT IN SEVERAL NETWORKS

Networking is all about sharing and exchanging ideas with people from different backgrounds. It can open up opportunities, expand knowledge, and create visibility for individuals.

Lena joined several networks, including the Global Entrepreneurship Network (GEN Global), the Women's Entrepreneurship Day Organisation (WEDO), the Leading Women of Africa (LWA), and the African Women in Leadership Organisation (AWLO). She attended several conferences organised by these organisations. She had the opportunity to sit and discuss with many hardworking and enlightened women who gave her the zeal to continue in what she was doing. She met many female motivational speakers who greatly inspired her. She gained insight into management techniques through several local and national workshops and seminars.

With little to no financial resources to execute projects, she created a social enterprise by bringing together all the groups she had established for the community under one strong network, known as the Tabwand Support Network. Because these groups work towards the same purpose and community, she restructured them to support each other economically, socially, and culturally. Through the creation of social ventures, they started solving some social and community problems together. The Women's Group, a member of this network, considered it a duty to raise funds to assist members of the Bui Disabled Persons Association (BDPA). The Nkumbiwa Development Forum (NDF), comprising young civil servants and professionals, served as mentors to all aspiring learners in the community and school drop-out members of Friends and Builders' Cooperative. The Tabwand Support Network has been changing lives by raising funds to support various projects, building the capacities of young women and girls through formal education and apprenticeships, supporting individuals with disabilities, and connecting people to other fruitful networks and partners.

Through the various networks, the other group members have acquired resources and property based on trust, due to the social bonding that continued to exist within the groups.

Today, the Tabwand Support Network is a recognised and registered civil society organisation in the books of the African Development Bank. It has empowered women in financial and digital literacy and boasts three food cooperatives and a financial cooperative.

Once you start something, create the habit of sticking to it. This requires consistency, patience, perseverance, and considerable effort on the part of the individual to succeed. In his book, *Tough Times Never Last, But Tough People Do*, Robert Schuller says that tough times are for tough people. "It is when you have gone through tough times that you become tough." After discovering herself, Lena had to build strategies for overcoming these challenges, which became an opportunity for her to grow.

EIGHT

The Crucible Moments that Led to the Bright Corridor

* * *

"You have to know who you are to grow your potential. But you have to grow in order to know who you are."

—John Maxwell

Y ou must pass through challenges to know who you are. Hard times are lessons for us.

Crucible moments are those pivotal moments or incidents that have had a profound impact and brought crucial lessons to Lena, helping to change her entire understanding of her purpose. These lessons, which have become her experiences, have provided her with the opportunities and steps to grow as a leader. Lena has never sat in a classroom as a student in leadership, but through her actions and achievements, she has discovered herself as a leader. What she used to think were difficulties and setbacks became a stepping stone for her growth.

All her mistakes, omissions and failures became great lessons for her. She decided to put in all the effort to improve herself continually. She learned when and how to be flexible and adaptable in the face of changes, in case things didn't turn out as expected. "There is always a silver lining in every dark cloud." The following crucial lessons keep Lena focused on the journey.

VISION IS A COMPASS

A vision is what gives us direction in everything we do. It helps us to determine where we are and where we are going. A clear vision, therefore, will help you to be focused. In fact, if you do not have a clear vision in life, you will face distractions that can take you off track. The members can have all the talents, resources and opportunities, but without a sense of direction, there will be no progress. Members who do not understand the vision tend to bring disorder. So, the vision should be well explained to the members.

From these lessons, Lena was able to carve out a clear vision that enabled her to move forward. Her entire purpose has been to provide value to women and young girls, ultimately improving their lives. She could now identify her itinerary, and her vision is now centred on adding value to others' lives. You must be able to bring something valuable to the people you value. You cannot give what you do not have.

If you don't know where you're going, you may not end up where you want to be. After acquiring some skills and experiences, she has been able to share them with her team, and her own stories have inspired many people. Myles Munroe says, "Your vision can take you to your destination."

At first, Lena had not mastered what she was offering to women and would mix things up. She could not track the record of her activities. After understanding the importance of her vision, she intentionally embarked on capacity building for the economic empowerment of women and young girls in the Kumbo community. She began to understand the reasons behind her actions, and everything fell into place. She could now clearly identify the potential in women. After attending the United Nations Women's Conference in New York in 2011, she learned the importance of creating a road map for every activity she had to carry out. In 2013, she visited the Ministry of Women's Empowerment and the Family in Yaounde several times to understand and master its mission and relationship to women. She integrated all her activities with those of women to suit the needs of this institution.

With the experiences from these structures, she could now focus on the program for Women's Economic Empowerment under the Sustainable Development Goals (Goal Five)

With a sense of direction, she began reading about influential people and attending various conferences and seminars that have helped her develop her leadership skills. She has been able to manage people and several difficult situations. She has continued to direct and guide several women and young girls of her community and beyond with empowering activities. She halted the trial-and-error way of managing issues. She has learnt to be continually creative and well-engaged in properly planning and preparing her activities, setting and evaluating small and achievable goals. She has been training most women on these principles to enable them to carry out their activities successfully.

A LEADER'S CHARACTER IS CRUCIAL

A leader must choose to be a better person. From a leader's character, we can determine the kind of person he/she is. A leader must develop a strong character to effectively influence and inspire their followers to work together. They must have the ability to guide and direct others. A leader's actions and intentions depend on the person's character. A leader must learn to be accountable for their actions. "Leadership is the capacity and will to rally men and women to a common purpose and the character which inspires confidence," said Bernard Montgomery, a British Field Marshal.

As a leader, you should learn to match your words with action, as this can significantly influence others. Your character will enable people to emulate you. You must not give promises that you cannot fulfil. You must be transparent, especially when it comes to money or finances. Whenever there is a problem, you must be able to analyse the situation and make decisions that can help to solve the problem. Members tend to respect the leader when they display certain values, such as consistency and responsibility. You must be a better leader for people to follow. Understanding that a leader's character is crucial, Lena learned to develop her own character as a leader through values such as self-discipline and honesty. She learned to love and support all those she has worked with, which has yielded fruit, as several people now believe in her actions.

Some people follow leaders because of what the leader has done. It is through the results of your actions that people begin to recognise you as their leader. That is when you are given the title of a good or bad leader. You gain the title of a good leader when you act positively. As John Maxwell says, "Your actions determine who you are." Talking and not acting will not make you a leader. A leader must put in those actions that will impact people's lives. He or she must make good decisions that will enable people to see the essence of life. If your actions demonstrate that you are genuinely out to help them and add value to their lives, they will believe in you and work with you. Most people do not want to be manipulated. Your actions should speak for themselves.

CONNECTING WITH PEOPLE MATTERS

From Lena's experiences, she has come to understand that people matter. A leader needs followers who are committed to the vision. Anyone who is a leader must have people following them. A leader cannot achieve their mission alone, so people play a significant part in the vision. She understood that leadership is about the people you are leading. According to John Maxwell, "If there are no people following you, then there is no leadership."

It is essential to foster strong and positive relationships with your followers. Working together with people can create an atmosphere of trust and collaboration.

Lena understood that as a leader, one must be able to work and collaborate with all followers, showing concern for everyone without discrimination. You must love and treat everyone with care, without which you will create discontent. You must be able to add value by training and educating them. A leader must be able to control and evaluate their team. When people know that you are there for them, have them at heart and can share in their pain and joy, they will trust you. When the leader gives people the proper honour and respect, they will trust the leader and reciprocate with respect. You will never do without people if you have to lead.

As the president of the Women's Group, Lena identified three distinct categories of women based on their behaviours and reactions to issues, especially during challenging moments.

The first category comprises women who cannot work or collaborate if no benefit is attached to their efforts. They cannot support or assist the group if they are not motivated. They must have something in return for what they have offered. For example, during our cultural events, members contribute money for food and drinks, but a member might want to eat a full plate and drink more than two bottles of beer because she contributed money, without considering the next person. Such women are always ready to throw slangs and criticise. They will never appreciate whatever you do and are always prepared to bring disorder. They will always devise strong reasons not to align with the group's rules and regulations. They are the first to drop out of the group for flimsy excuses.

The second category consists of women who are extremely loyal to the group. They are ready and willing to work for the group without any motivation. They are prepared to sacrifice their time and energy for the group's success and are ready to support the group financially or morally without complaining. These are very committed members who will collaborate until the end. Despite the challenges, they are ready to go the extra mile for the group's success.

The third category of women consists of those who are unable to make decisions on their own. They are simply following the crowd. If most members oppose, they will oppose; if they are not complaining, they will also stay quiet. They are always sitting on the fence. When given a task, they complete it without complaint, but if they are prompted to do so, they will indirectly complain and create problems that they cannot even resolve if left to their own devices.

At first, it was difficult for Lena to work with these different groups of people. She thought she should only work with her own friends. Still, after several challenges, she began applying the Pareto Principle, which suggests that eighty per cent of one's time and energy should be devoted to building the top twenty per cent of people who can produce excellent and satisfactory results. The remaining twenty per cent of one's time and energy is to uplift the rest of the people. This principle has been a booster to her way of managing people. She grasped through the hard way that as a leader, you are obliged to work with everyone, even with your enemies. It is also beneficial to educate those who do not share our perspective.

EFFECTIVE COMMUNICATION IS NECESSARY

Effective communication establishes the vision and image of the group. The way you communicate with people must create an impact. It took Lena time to understand that what you say and how you say it matters. It is necessary to give a clear explanation of what you are doing. You must believe in what you say and say the truth to connect with the people. When you share the right knowledge and ideas with your people, they will believe in and trust you. People in your network will always share your vision if it is well communicated. Members must understand the goals and objectives of the group. It is only through regular communication that people can master the rules and regulations of the group.

It is the leader's responsibility to ensure that there is feedback on every issue, which will promote the group's good functioning. A leader should be able to identify what is working and what is not within the group and carefully explain this to the members to avoid misunderstandings. After many challenges, Lena realised that it was beneficial to open up, as honest communication is essential for solving problems. It creates an atmosphere of transparency and mutual trust. Communicating with team members puts everyone on the same page for the group's success.

Communicating with people is also about listening and understanding them. It makes them feel valued and worthy. It shows respect, and it is a way of building good relationships with people. Listening to other people's ideas, whether good or bad, will also enable you to increase your knowledge.

Lena also understood that people love to be listened to. When you take the time to listen to them, they build confidence in you and will be more likely to confide in you. It took Lena time to understand the value of listening to other people's ideas and opinions. She has now learned that when you listen more, you gain a lot of insight into the issues surrounding you.

PERSONAL VALUES ARE GREAT POTENTIALS

Personal values and beliefs can shape an individual's character and behaviour. They can help the individual make good or bad decisions. An individual's values and actions can enable others to determine the authenticity of the individual and their actions. Lena's values and what she stands for have built her strength.

Her values helped her to master and understand herself

- Lena improved herself as a leader through the four "Ds" and four "Cs"
- Discipline- Determination- Dedication- Diligence.
- Courage- Concentration- Commitment- Consistency.

In fact, she altered her perception of herself and others, as well as how she views the world. Being disciplined is essential for managing oneself and others. She had to develop her own system for managing herself more effectively. Putting priorities first has been her mantra. There is no need to program many things when you know you will not accomplish them. When leading, it is essential to avoid making unnecessary excuses. Some women fail to carry out important tasks because of a lack of self–discipline. They will not respect the rules and regulations and will continue to provide unnecessary excuses. When you are a disciplined leader, people believe in you and trust you. A good leader must be determined to work hard and accept responsibilities. You must be ready to adopt the "*Get it well done*" attitude and face whatever happens, especially the difficulties and challenges that arise from your actions. With this in mind, Lena did everything to pick up the broken pieces of whatever difficulty she encountered. She has had to restructure some of the groups she created several times.

Dedicating your time, energy, and resources is part of this journey. You must be prepared to persevere even when things are tough, because your vision is worth fighting for; therefore, you need to be dedicated to it.

When leading, one should be courageous enough to direct and guide others to make positive decisions that will impact their lives. A show of courage will enable you to face challenges and set things right, so people can have confidence in you. You must be ready to go the extra mile. Being a courageous leader will inspire others around you and make them committed to whatever they do in life. Due to her courage, Lena successfully navigated the financial and leadership crisis in the Women's Group.

Commitment comes from the heart and is all about engagement and involvement. This helped Lena and her vision, and she learned to do whatever it takes to keep her vision alive. It needs that strong willpower to keep going. Being committed will help to inspire and attract other people. Being committed tends to foster strong relationships and collaboration with members because it demonstrates to your followers that you are serious, and they can emulate your style. You must be ready and intentional to follow up on the activities of your group till the end.

Consistency will help you to monitor the progress of your activities. Many things can be achieved if you, as a leader, can remain consistent in your approach. When you consistently participate in the group activities, people will believe in you, and your goals will be achieved. Your daily habits and routine practices are of prime importance. You must make every effort to master the small processes within your organisation. You must start with little issues and then develop them to grow. You must develop the habit of always being present and engaged in your activities, as it helps you identify potential pitfalls or loopholes. This enables you to understand the team better and identify those who merit reward or recognition.

Her Values helped her to build a strong relationship with people

Through respect and honesty, you can earn the trust of your people, which in turn fosters good relationships among them. Respect is reciprocal because you will also be respected when you respect others. Lena encountered a situation in the Women's Group where an elderly woman complained that the young girls were not respecting them, and a young girl replied that the elderly women were not respecting them as well. It is necessary to respect the elders, but sometimes the elders must also show respect to deserve respect.

When you are trusted, you become motivated to do more and build good ties to achieve good results. You must earn the trust of the people you lead to avoid unnecessary conflicts. For example, because of the transparency in handling the group's finances, the person in charge will earn the trust of other members. When there is trust and transparency in a team, people work well.

Cultivating a spirit of gratitude is crucial for a leader. You must show appreciation to hard-working members for their achievements through rewards. You must learn to recognise all those who have continued to work tirelessly, those in your inner circle who have adhered to the group's principles and remain loyal to the vision. In the Women's Group, hard-working women are recognised every five years.

Her values enabled her to create a good working environment

When people are motivated, they work together. A leader who believes in fairness and honesty will create a collaborative and peaceful atmosphere in a group. You must be honest, accept your mistakes, and remain accountable for your actions. This fosters a positive working environment where people feel comfortable opening up to one another. When you do the right thing or take honest decisions, people will be motivated to work with you. Your attitude should serve as an inspiration to your followers. Even when the going is tough, it's essential to maintain a sense of optimism and hope to face the challenges.

NINE

Becoming a Woman of Influence

* * *

"A woman of influence is a woman who can embrace leadership roles, and aspire to make a significant and influential impact at work, in a business, and in a community because she desires to create a better world for herself and the future generation."
—Becca Powers, *Harness Your Inner CEO*

A woman of influence is a model or exemplary person, a person of integrity. If you place your priorities correctly, maintain a positive attitude, and practice self-discipline, you can become a person of influence to others. You must also be accountable and take responsibility for your actions.

As a woman of influence, knowing your temperaments, talents, strengths, and weaknesses is necessary. You must know how to create awareness and address the challenging issues that make work difficult for you. It is vital to acquire problem-solving skills, build courage, have self-confidence, and learn to face life's realities. Having a positive self-image, letting go of life's setbacks, and learning to avoid self-limiting beliefs can be a significant boost to one's self-image. Being honest and truthful makes you a transparent person. You should learn to accept that you are responsible for your own actions and attitude. With all of this, people will see you as someone they can count on, which makes you feel like a role model. As a woman of influence, you must be someone with good character. You need to know that people follow you to emulate you. If you can create something for people to look forward to and help unlock their potential, you have made a lasting impact in their lives, and you will be regarded as a leader with influence.

Lena believes it is essential to have a positive mindset that enables you to inspire others. Through the transformational, servant, and pace-setting leadership styles, Lena has created a life of significance for several people, especially women and young girls. She has been able to connect with them through her numerous actions.

Lena realised that several women listened to her and worked with her for various reasons and from various angles, creating influence.

For example, some women stayed on the journey with her because they understood who Lena was—a person who must produce results, an authentic person who will match words with actions. It may be because she shares the same personality traits as they, as it is said that birds of the same feather flock together.

Another group of women listened to and worked with her because of her vision and leadership skills. From her initiatives, they acquired knowledge and skills that have changed their lives. They have developed several competencies and can enhance their chances of starting their own businesses. The workshops and training she organised empowered them and added value to their lives. For this reason, they are still on the journey.

Some have stayed on the journey because Lena has navigated their difficulties with them, and they have overcome them together. Some have received her financial, material, and moral support, which has changed their lives.

This other group of women listened to and worked with her because they were in her inner circle. Because of their loyalty, they had to stick with her wherever she went and whatever she did. They believed in her despite her weaknesses. Today, they remain together on their journey because of their enduring love for each other.

Another group of women listened to and worked with her due to her long-standing position as president of the Women's Group. They had to listen and work with her because they were obliged by the group's rules and regulations to respect her authority, so she could influence them.

After overcoming the challenges, discovering herself, her values, and her personality, and realising the importance of some leadership roles, Lena can now boast of being a woman of influence. This has given her the energy and strong will to connect with herself and intentionally apply some basic leadership principles, styles, skills, and practices she has acquired along the way. She still has the edge to continue developing other leaders, impacting and influencing as many people as possible.

This enabled Lena to continue her leadership journey with a strong will to mobilise potential leaders, empower their abilities, equip them with leadership tools, and build good relationships and strong networks that will help them grow, impact, and influence others in their communities as authentic next-generation leaders for better lives, known as the BERLA PILLARS OF GROWTH. This presents another challenge for her because it is not easy to practise what you preach.

Through the Berla Pillars of Growth, Lena will continue to build, connect and transform the lives of as many people as possible in her community and beyond in line with the following missions under the acronym BERLA (Building Economic Resilience and Leadership for Aspiring Young People).

Lena's first mission as a woman of influence is to bring young people together and enable them to discover their potential by serving as mobilisers

Lena will first have to identify their capabilities as leaders to bring them together. They will be encouraged to think outside the box and develop growth and creative mindsets to build themselves. Many people, especially women, are incredibly talented but often unaware of their worth. They are not aware of what they have and who they are. Most of them are not able to identify their potential. They do not believe in themselves. Because they lack self-confidence, they cannot achieve their goals. They are limited in several areas. It is essential to help them understand who they are, their significance, and their value. Training them to work together is essential because it enables them to understand each other's strengths and weaknesses. It will be necessary for Lena to look into all the processes and procedures for bringing these youths together.

Bringing them together can enhance social bonding and foster more meaningful social interactions. If shown respect and love, they can feel a sense of belonging and security. After bringing them together, Lena will have to set principles to understand where they are and where they want to go.

Lena's second mission as a woman of influence is to "equip and empower" people by serving as a mentor

It means regularly meeting with identified potential individuals to build their capacities and enable them to acquire the skills necessary for their lives.

To build people's capabilities, you must identify those with the potential who need improvement. It is not enough to tell people what they should do. You must help them acquire the necessary skills and knowledge. Some people are eager to learn, and some do not care. You must choose those who are committed, willing, and ready to learn and possess the necessary abilities. You can model and motivate everyone, but you must select those you want to mentor because you cannot mentor someone who is uninterested. When you help people develop their gifts and talents, it can transform their lives, as they will acquire new skills and enhance their potential and capacity for growth. People will not follow someone with no skills or knowledge about what they are doing. *"When you expand others, you also expand yourself,"* John Maxwell.

There are always people who face difficulties, and they will always need others to support and guide them as they navigate these challenges. As a woman of influence, you should be prepared to support others through life's challenges. You must understand their strengths and weaknesses. You must be able to identify the person's blind spots, where they are falling short, and whether they are reaching their full potential. This will enable you to understand the person you want to help, determine whether they are struggling, and provide support to uplift them.

Empowering people means helping them see what they can do without you and giving them the authority to do it. Everyone needs a place to belong. You need to trust them with the tasks so that they can complete them independently. Empowering your people enables you to help them take responsibility for their own development.

Lena's philosophy has been to encourage every young girl to "create something and own something." Lena has applied this philosophy to create several structures, including the Career-Advancement Women's Entrepreneurship Champions Organisation (CAWEECO), the BERLA Meridian Group, BERLA Channels, the Women's Leadership Arena, and the Men Should Lead Forum. These platforms have become great channels for empowering people in leadership and personal development. Lena has utilized several leadership programs, incorporating her stories and experiences, to mentor and coach these young girls and boys. She has been encouraging all of them to pursue the option of innovation and creativity, as this can open up many opportunities for their success in life. Lena keeps advising them to read books, attend conferences, and participate in seminars and workshops because these events inspired her to take on new challenges, and she hopes they can be inspired as well.

These leadership trainings have enabled young girls to build strong connections with their peers and other adult learners. They have created dynamism and a vibrant momentum in their different communities and sectors of life. When you effectively communicate a clear vision, it will attract people, and once they discover that they are on the right path, they will stick to it. They will be able to solve their own problems, boost their performance, and drive their own growth.

Lena's third mission as a woman of influence is to "relate" with people to build strong and fruitful relationships and networks by being a motivator

When people feel valued and cared for, they build trust in the leader. You must be someone people enjoy working with. It is said that people tend to associate with those they get along with. You do not try to rule with a stick but with a personal touch. As a person of influence, you must learn to demonstrate the love and willingness to help others grow and become better. A leader needs to listen to people, observe them, learn from their situations, and guide them effectively. When a leader has good motives for working with people, the people will also work with the leader in a genuine atmosphere. As an effective leader, you must always consider the needs and perspectives of others.

One can only succeed in connecting with people if there is love. People should feel that they have love and support. When you focus on serving others, you have their trust. Therefore, take the time to express love and appreciation to the people around you. People will increase their willingness to do the work they are supposed to perform. When you show care for people, they will be more willing to initiate new projects and remain committed.

A humble leader who values people doesn't promote themselves but promotes others, because leadership is not about the leader, but about the people. When you treat people with respect, you also receive respect. People love it when their opinions are also considered. A leader who listens to others is respected and trusted. Because of these qualities, the people will build a collaborative attitude. When people understand that you are someone who seeks to know about their problems and can stand by your words, they will see that they are safe.

As a woman of influence, you should treat others the way you would like to be treated. Always try to determine what matters most to your people. Look for ways to celebrate and recognise the people for a well-done job. You must always create a conducive environment for your workers. You should learn to encourage your people and let them feel comfortable with themselves, and they will never forget about you. It is very necessary to support them. When people believe their leader is always with them during their good and bad moments, they are more likely to work for the organisation's benefit. We must help people change their attitudes and build good relationships to lead their families, grow their businesses, and interact with others. These are very sound principles that Lena has been using to attract her followers.

Lena's fourth mission as a woman of influence is to develop others to lead by being a team builder

After identifying their potential, equipping and empowering them, they should be able to move forward and take on leadership responsibilities. Because one cannot work alone, one must learn to work with others as a team. Leadership abilities are essential for developing other leaders. You must be committed and able to train others who are ready to carry on what you have taught them. They will become influencers and the next-generation leaders. They are expected to pass on what they have received from you and what they have learned on their own. When you help others become leaders, you transform their approach to interacting with others. If they become good leaders, you have not only changed their lives but also those of the people they encounter.

At the Berla Channels International Centre (BCIC) for Skills

Development, Lena introduced the Berla Culture to young leaders. The leaders are trained to build strong values that will enable them to be committed and consistently champion, teach, practise, and reward leadership. It is about people who are willing and eager to use their knowledge, skills, and time to make meaningful contributions to others' lives. When you teach others what you know, they will, in turn, teach others what they know and what they received from you. With this circle, they will continue to spread ideas and the vision. Through the Berla Channels Training Programs, Lena is prepared and determined to pass the leadership baton to young people who are truly committed to continuing the race.

Lena's fifth mission as a woman of influence is about being authentic by serving as a role model

Her dream of giving back to the community has compelled her to become an inspiration and a model to people from other communities. Having understood who she is, this mission is to establish an authentic image of leadership and demonstrate the best attitude towards people. Everyone must realise that authenticity is the key to success in leadership. A leader must remain genuine in all their activities. In leadership, action is imperative. It is all about being relevant and genuine in what you say and do. You should learn to align your words and actions with the leadership principles and rules. We all need to be sincere and accountable as leaders. We tend to give more to society when we believe in our values and passion. This will enable us to build good relationships with friends and family. We must promote this authentic way of doing things. To be a role model, you must be willing to develop yourself and others continually.

CONCLUSION

* * *

Because leadership is a process and a journey that must continue, leaving a legacy is important. You must be ready to pass on the knowledge, skills, and competencies you have acquired throughout the years. The race baton must be handed over to a person prepared to run more than the person handing over the baton. It is therefore necessary to develop other people who will carry on the vision. This inspired Lena to create several platforms where she has been building other leaders, whose responsibilities include teaching others for continuity.

The dream of giving back to the community has changed her way of thinking, her feelings, and her actions. Lena thought it was to help people escape their demise, but she only realised later that it is a long journey with all the uncertainties, difficulties, and opportunities. Somewhere along the journey, things were so bleak, but with her never-give-up attitude, the journey continued, and through all the setbacks, she discovered herself and what she was meant to do. The reality of the dream has compelled Lena to become an inspiration and a model to people from other communities.

The 60 Leadership Qualities that Define Effective Leaders

* * *

"Management is doing things right. Leadership is doing the right things."
—Peter Drucker, Management Consultant, Educator, & Author

Behind every transformative decision, every groundbreaking innovation, and every act that shapes our world stands a leader. But what makes one leader stand tall while others fade into the background?

It's more than just strategy or decision-making process; it's a symphony of practical, subtle, profound leadership qualities that come together in harmony. Effective leadership is about creating a vision, inspiring others, making informed decisions, and ultimately guiding a team towards achieving their collective goals. Understanding what makes a leader effective can be a game-changer for any individual or organisation, providing the stepping stone towards success and excellence. What is effective leadership? Effective leadership is the ability to turn a vision into reality by encouraging others to follow you on a shared journey.

It is the art and science of guiding a group towards a shared goal. Effective leadership is not a static characteristic or single defining trait. Rather, it's a collection of qualities that evolve. It goes beyond mere management; it also involves inspiring and motivating a team, fostering a positive and conducive work environment, and making strategic decisions that benefit an organisation. It's about fostering a sense of unity and collaboration. A good leader ensures that every team member feels valued, heard, and integral to the team's success. They are skilled at harnessing the collective strengths of their team and channelling them towards achieving common objectives. In essence, leadership can be likened to an orchestra conductor, coordinating various instruments to produce harmonious music.

WHY IS EFFECTIVE LEADERSHIP IMPORTANT?

Effective leadership is the backbone of any successful organisation or team. Good leaders are instrumental in ensuring efficient operations and contributing to the overall success of businesses. They wield a strong influence over their team members' morale, motivation, and job satisfaction, which in turn fuels productivity and innovation. A competent leader can inspire a team to achieve feats they never thought possible, pushing the boundaries of their potential. The qualities of a leader also play a crucial role in navigating change and tackling challenges. Whether it's a shift in market trends, a transition in organisational structure, or a global crisis, effective leaders are the lighthouses that guide their teams safely through the turbulent seas of change. Their resilience, adaptability, and strategic foresight are pivotal in ensuring stability and continuity in times of uncertainty.

WHAT ARE THE 60 KEY ELEMENTS OF EFFECTIVE LEADERSHIP?

To be an effective leader, one must possess unique qualities and skills that set them apart. Understanding and developing these qualities can significantly enhance your leadership abilities and positively impact those around you, so let's dive into the 60 key elements of effective leadership!

1. EFFECTIVE COMMUNICATION

Effective communication is an essential tool for successful leadership. It involves clearly conveying thoughts, ideas, and expectations to team members and actively listening to their feedback and concerns. Good leaders create an open and transparent environment where everyone feels comfortable sharing their thoughts and opinions. By fostering effective communication, leaders ensure that information flows freely, ideas are shared, and the team feels heard and valued.

2. EMOTIONAL INTELLIGENCE

Emotional intelligence refers to the ability to recognise, understand, and manage one's own emotions and those of others. Leaders with high emotional intelligence can empathise with their team members, respond to their needs, and maintain strong interpersonal relationships. This quality enables leaders to create a supportive and inclusive work environment where everyone feels valued and motivated to contribute their best.

3. INTEGRITY

Integrity is a fundamental quality of effective leaders. They uphold strong ethical standards, act honestly, and demonstrate consistency between their words and actions. Leaders with integrity build trust within their team, as their team members feel confident that they can rely on their leader's honesty and fairness. By fostering a culture of trust, leaders create an environment where collaboration and open communication thrive.

4. ACCOUNTABILITY

Effective leaders take responsibility for their own actions and decisions, as well as those of their team. They hold themselves and their team members accountable for achieving goals and meeting expectations. By demonstrating accountability, leaders foster a culture of ownership and commitment, resulting in increased engagement and productivity.

5. DECISION-MAKING

Good decision-making is a crucial aspect of effective leadership. Leaders must be able to analyse situations, consider different perspectives, and weigh the risks and benefits before deciding. Decisive leaders are not afraid to make tough choices, even in challenging or uncertain circumstances. They understand the importance of taking action and providing clarity to their team, instilling confidence and maintaining momentum.

6. CONFIDENCE

Confidence is a key quality of effective leaders. They believe in their abilities and their team's potential. Confident leaders inspire trust and respect from their team members, enabling them to lead with authority and conviction. By demonstrating confidence, leaders create an environment where team members feel empowered and motivated to achieve their best.

7. PROBLEM-SOLVING

Effective leaders possess strong problem-solving skills. They can identify challenges, analyse the root causes, and develop creative solutions to overcome obstacles. By demonstrating resilience and adaptability, leaders can navigate challenges and drive their team to success.

8. CREATIVITY

Creativity is an essential quality for effective leadership. Leaders who think creatively can generate innovative ideas, strategies, and solutions to address challenges and drive growth. By fostering a culture of innovation and continuous improvement, creative leaders inspire their team members to think outside the box and contribute their unique perspectives and talents.

9. SELF-AWARENESS

Self-awareness is the ability to recognise and understand one's own strengths, weaknesses, emotions, and motivations. Effective leaders are self-aware, which enables them to make informed decisions, manage their emotions, and adapt their leadership style to different situations and team dynamics. By being self-aware, leaders can continuously learn and grow, enhancing their leadership effectiveness and positively impacting their team and organisation.

10. GOAL SETTING

Effective leaders set clear, achievable goals for themselves and their team. They understand the importance of having a vision and establishing objectives that align with the organisation's mission and values. By setting goals, leaders provide direction and focus, enabling their team to work together towards a common purpose and measure their progress along the way.

11. DELEGATION

Delegation is a critical skill for effective leadership. Leaders must be able to assign tasks and responsibilities to their team members based on their strengths and capabilities. By delegating effectively, leaders empower their team members, allowing them to grow, develop, and contribute to the organisation's success.

12. HUMILITY

Humility is an essential quality of effective leaders. They recognise that they do not have all the answers and are open to learning from others. Humble leaders appreciate the contributions of their team members and are willing to admit their mistakes and learn from them. By demonstrating humility, leaders create an environment where everyone feels valued and respected, fostering collaboration and continuous improvement.

13. ACTIVE LISTENING

Active listening is a vital skill for effective leadership. It involves fully engaging with and understanding the speaker's message, asking clarifying questions, and providing feedback. Leaders who actively listen to their team members demonstrate empathy and respect, fostering trust and open communication.

14. RESILIENCE

Resilience is the ability to bounce back from setbacks and adapt to changing circumstances. Effective leaders are resilient, maintaining a positive attitude and remaining focused on their goals despite challenges and obstacles. By demonstrating resilience, leaders inspire their team members to persevere and stay committed to their objectives.

15. CONTINUOUS LEARNING

Effective leaders are committed to continuous learning and personal growth. They seek opportunities to expand their knowledge, skills, and experiences, and encourage their team members to do the same. By fostering a culture of learning, leaders ensure that their team stays adaptable and prepared for the ever-changing business landscape.

16. STRATEGY DEVELOPMENT

Successful leaders can develop and implement effective strategies to achieve their goals. They can analyse the current situation, identify opportunities and threats, and create a roadmap for success. By developing a clear strategy, leaders provide direction and focus for their team, ensuring that everyone is working towards a common objective.

17. HONESTY

Honesty is a fundamental quality of effective leaders. They are truthful and transparent in their communication, fostering trust and credibility within their team. By being honest, leaders create an environment where team members feel comfortable sharing their thoughts and opinions, leading to better collaboration and decision-making.

18. MOTIVATION

Effective leaders can motivate and inspire their team members. They understand what drives each individual and create an environment where everyone feels engaged and committed to their work. By providing encouragement, recognition, and support, leaders help their team members achieve their full potential and contribute to the organisation's success.

19. CONFLICT RESOLUTION

Conflict resolution is an essential skill for effective leadership. Leaders must be able to address and resolve conflicts within their team, ensuring that everyone feels heard and respected. Leaders create a harmonious work environment by effectively managing conflicts, where collaboration and productivity can thrive.

20. TRANSPARENCY

Transparency is a key element of effective leadership. Leaders who are transparent in their communication and decision-making processes build trust within their team and create an environment where everyone feels informed and included. By being transparent, leaders foster open communication and collaboration, leading to better decision-making and overall team performance.

21. EMPATHY

Empathy is the ability to understand and share the feelings of others. Effective leaders demonstrate empathy by acknowledging the emotions and perspectives of their team members and responding with compassion and support. By showing empathy, leaders create a supportive and inclusive work environment where everyone feels valued and motivated to contribute their best.

22. DECISIVENESS

Decisiveness is a critical quality of effective leaders. They can make timely and well-informed decisions, even in the face of uncertainty or limited information. Decisive leaders provide clarity and direction for their team, instilling confidence and ensuring that progress is made towards their goals.

23. POSITIVITY

Positivity is an essential attribute of effective leaders. They maintain an optimistic outlook, focusing on opportunities and potential for growth, even in challenging situations. By demonstrating positivity, leaders inspire their team members to adopt a similar mindset, fostering a culture of enthusiasm and motivation.

24. PASSION

Passion is a key quality of effective leaders. They are deeply committed to their work and genuinely care about the success of their team and organisation. By demonstrating passion, leaders inspire their team members to share in their enthusiasm and dedication, creating a highly motivated and engaged workforce.

25. ADAPTABILITY

Adaptability is the ability to adjust to changing circumstances and embrace new challenges. Effective leaders are flexible and open to change, recognising that evolving situations may require different approaches. By being adaptable, leaders can navigate through uncertainty and guide their team towards success.

26. VISION

Effective leaders have a clear vision for the future and can communicate it to their team. They inspire and motivate their team members to work towards a common goal, providing direction and purpose. With a strong vision, leaders can drive innovation and growth within their organisation.

27. COLLABORATION

Collaboration is a critical aspect of effective leadership. Leaders who foster a collaborative work environment encourage their team members to share ideas, knowledge, and resources. By promoting teamwork and cooperation, leaders can ensure their team is more efficient, innovative, and successful.

28. INFLUENCE

Influence is the ability to persuade and inspire others to follow your lead. Effective leaders possess strong influencing skills, enabling them to gain the support and commitment of their team members. By being influential, leaders can drive change and achieve their goals more effectively.

29. PATIENCE

Patience is an essential quality of effective leaders. They understand that success takes time and are willing to invest effort and resources to achieve their goals. By being patient, leaders can maintain a long-term perspective and avoid making hasty decisions that may have negative consequences.

30. APPROACHABILITY

Approachability is being accessible and open to communication with team members. Effective leaders create an environment where their team members feel comfortable discussing concerns, ideas, and feedback. By being approachable, leaders can foster trust, open communication, and a strong team dynamic.

31. TIME MANAGEMENT

Effective leaders are skilled at managing their time and prioritising tasks. They can balance the demands of their role, ensuring that they allocate sufficient time to strategic planning, decision-making, and team development. By managing their time effectively, leaders can maximise their productivity and achieve their goals more efficiently.

32. COACHING AND MENTORING

Effective leaders are committed to the growth and development of their team members. They provide coaching and mentoring, helping their team members to enhance their skills, overcome challenges, and achieve their full potential. By investing in the development of their team, leaders can ensure long-term success and sustainability for their organisation.

33. CULTURAL AWARENESS

Cultural awareness is the ability to recognise, understand, and appreciate team members' diverse backgrounds, beliefs, and values. Effective leaders are culturally aware, promoting inclusivity and respect within their team. By being culturally aware, leaders can create a supportive and diverse work environment where everyone feels valued and can contribute their best.

34. RISK MANAGEMENT

Effective leaders are skilled at identifying and managing risks. They can assess potential threats and opportunities, develop contingency plans, and make informed decisions to minimise negative impacts. By being proactive in risk management, leaders can ensure the stability and success of their organisation.

35. NETWORKING

Networking is building and maintaining relationships with individuals and organisations that can support the leader's goals and objectives. Effective leaders are skilled at networking strategically, leveraging their connections to access resources, information, and opportunities. Leaders can enhance their influence and drive positive organisational outcomes by cultivating a strong network.

36. INITIATIVE

Initiative is taking charge and acting proactively to address challenges and seize opportunities. Effective leaders demonstrate initiative by identifying areas for improvement, proposing solutions, and driving change. By taking the initiative, leaders can create momentum and inspire their team to achieve their goals.

37. FOCUS

Focus is concentrating on the most critical tasks and objectives, avoiding distractions and maintaining a clear sense of direction. Effective leaders are focused, ensuring their team remains aligned with the organisation's goals and priorities. By maintaining focus, leaders can drive efficiency and productivity, ensuring that their team achieves its full potential.

38. ASSERTIVENESS

Assertiveness is the ability to express one's thoughts, opinions, and needs confidently and respectfully. Effective leaders are assertive, enabling them to communicate their expectations clearly and address issues directly and effectively. By being assertive, leaders can create an environment of open communication and mutual respect within their team.

39. DIPLOMACY

Diplomacy is the ability to navigate complex situations and relationships tactfully and sensitively. Effective leaders are diplomatic, gracefully managing conflicts and disagreements and finding solutions that satisfy all parties. By being diplomatic, leaders can maintain harmony within their team and foster positive relationships with stakeholders.

40. PERSEVERANCE

Perseverance is the ability to persist in the face of obstacles and setbacks, maintaining a steadfast commitment to one's goals. Effective leaders demonstrate perseverance, inspiring their team to remain resilient and focused on achieving their objectives. By being persistent, leaders can drive their team towards success and overcome challenges that may arise.

41. CRITICAL THINKING

Critical thinking is analysing information, evaluating

evidence, and making logical decisions based on objective rea-
soning. Effective leaders possess strong critical thinking skills,
enabling them to make informed decisions and solve complex
problems. By applying critical thinking, leaders can identify
the best course of action and drive their team towards success.

42. EMOTIONAL STABILITY

Emotional stability is the ability to maintain composure and
self-control in challenging situations. Effective leaders demonstrate emotional stability, managing their emotions and reactions
in a way that promotes a positive work environment. By being
emotionally stable, leaders can provide consistent guidance and
support to their team, even in times of stress or uncertainty.

43. SENSE OF HUMOUR

A sense of humour is the ability to appreciate and share
humour, creating a light-hearted and enjoyable atmosphere.
Effective leaders possess a sense of humour, using it to diffuse
tension, build rapport, and maintain a positive work environment. By incorporating humour, leaders can foster strong team
dynamics and improve morale.

44. APPRECIATION AND RECOGNITION

Appreciation and recognition involve acknowledging team
members' hard work, achievements, and contributions. Effective leaders express genuine appreciation and recognise their
team's efforts, fostering a culture of gratitude and motivation.
By showing appreciation and recognition, leaders can boost
morale, increase job satisfaction, and encourage continued high
performance.

45. AGILITY

Agility is the ability to respond quickly and effectively to changing circumstances, embracing new challenges and opportunities. Effective leaders are agile, adapting their strategies and approaches as needed to ensure continued success. By being nimble, leaders can navigate through uncertainty and maintain a competitive edge in a rapidly evolving business landscape.

46. EMPOWERMENT

Empowerment involves giving team members the authority, resources, and support to take ownership of their work and make decisions. Effective leaders empower their team, fostering a sense of autonomy and responsibility. By empowering their team members, leaders can foster innovation, enhance engagement, and achieve better results.

47. COMPASSION

Compassion is the ability to genuinely care and show concern for the well-being of others. Effective leaders demonstrate compassion, understanding their team members' challenges and offering support when needed. By being compassionate, leaders can foster a supportive work environment where team members feel valued and cared for, leading to increased job satisfaction and performance.

48. CHARISMA

Charisma is the ability to inspire and captivate others through one's personality and presence. Effective leaders possess charisma, enabling them to connect more deeply with their team members and stakeholders. By being charismatic, leaders can motivate and influence others, driving positive outcomes for their organisation.

49. CONSISTENCY

Consistency involves maintaining a steady and reliable approach to leadership, ensuring that actions, decisions, and communication are aligned with the organisation's values and goals. Effective leaders consistently provide their team with a stable and predictable environment. By being consistent, leaders can build trust, credibility, and a strong team culture.

50. CURIOSITY

Curiosity is the desire to learn, explore, and seek new information or experiences. Effective leaders are curious, constantly seeking opportunities to expand their knowledge and improve their skills. By fostering a culture of curiosity, leaders can encourage innovation, drive continuous improvement, and ensure their team remains adaptable in a rapidly changing world.

51. TRUSTWORTHINESS

Trustworthiness is a crucial quality for effective leaders. It is built through consistent actions, honesty, and reliability. Trustworthy leaders keep their promises, demonstrate integrity, and communicate transparently. Leaders foster strong relationships, open dialogue, and collaboration by cultivating trust within their team.

52. OPEN-MINDEDNESS

Effective leaders are open to new ideas, perspectives, and feedback. They create an inclusive environment where team members feel comfortable sharing their thoughts and opinions. Open-minded leaders value diversity and recognise that innovative solutions can emerge from different viewpoints. They actively seek input from their team members, consider alternative approaches, and adapt their strategies accordingly.

53. FLEXIBILITY

Leaders must be adaptable in their approach. They understand that situations and circumstances can change, necessitating adjustments to their strategies or plans. Effective leaders remain agile and adaptable, continually embracing new information and adjusting their course of action as needed. Flexibility allows leaders to navigate challenges, seize opportunities, and maintain forward momentum.

54. ACTIVE ENGAGEMENT

Active engagement involves actively involving team members in decision-making processes, discussions, and problem-solving. Effective leaders promote active engagement, ensuring that everyone has a voice and feels valued in the team. By fostering active engagement, leaders can tap into the collective wisdom of their team, leading to better decision-making and enhanced team performance.

55. SELF-DISCIPLINE

Self-discipline is the ability to control one's impulses, emotions, and actions to achieve desired outcomes. Effective leaders demonstrate self-discipline, consistently working towards their goals and maintaining focus despite distractions or setbacks. By practising self-discipline, leaders can serve as role models for their team members and cultivate a culture of commitment and perseverance.

56. STRATEGIC THINKING

Strategic thinking involves analysing complex situations, identifying patterns and trends, and developing long-term plans to achieve desired outcomes. Effective leaders possess strong strategic thinking skills, enabling them to guide their team and organisation towards a successful future. By thinking strategically, leaders can anticipate challenges, seize opportunities, and ensure the long-term sustainability of their organisation.

57. FEEDBACK AND CONSTRUCTIVE CRITICISM

Effective leaders understand the importance of providing feedback and constructive criticism to their team members. They are skilled at delivering feedback in a supportive and actionable manner, focusing on growth and development. By offering constructive criticism, leaders can help their team members improve their performance, learn from mistakes, and reach their full potential.

58. RESOURCEFULNESS

Resourcefulness is the ability to find quick and clever ways to overcome difficulties or challenges. Effective leaders are resourceful, utilising their creativity and problem-solving skills to find innovative solutions to obstacles. By being resourceful, leaders can maximise the use of available resources, drive efficiency, and achieve their goals more effectively.

59. COURAGE

Courage is facing challenges, taking risks, and making difficult decisions despite fear or uncertainty. Effective leaders demonstrate courage by standing up for their beliefs and taking action, even when it may be unpopular or risky. By exhibiting courage, leaders can inspire their team members to embrace challenges and push their boundaries, ultimately driving growth and success.

60. DEALING WITH AMBIGUITY

Dealing with ambiguity involves navigating uncertainty, making decisions, and taking action even when information is incomplete or unclear. Effective leaders are skilled at dealing with ambiguity, remaining adaptable and resilient in the face of changing circumstances. By being comfortable with ambiguity, leaders can guide their team through uncertain situations and maintain progress towards their goals.

About the Author

* * *

Dr. Bertha Yiberla Yenwo is a pioneering social entrepreneur, leadership coach, business counsellor, and certified Project Management Office (PMO) practitioner. As the founder and CEO of the Mike Denny International Institute of Excellence in Cameroon, she is widely recognised for her work in empowering women and promoting inclusive leadership.

Dr. Yenwo holds a Bachelor's degree in Law from the University of Yaounde and a Higher Diploma from the prestigious National School of Administration and Magistracy (ENAM),

Yaoundé. She also holds an Honorary Doctorate (Honoris Causa) in Social Service from the Socrates Social Research University Trust. Her professional excellence has earned her multiple leadership awards.

Overcoming early challenges with self-confidence, Dr. Yenwo has become a beacon of transformation, fuelled by a commitment to self-education and empowerment. Guided by her personal philosophy—"Create Something – Own Something"—she has led numerous initiatives focused on leadership, personal development, entrepreneurship, financial and digital literacy, and financial inclusion for women and underserved communities.

Her impactful contributions include the founding of several key initiatives and organisations:

- Berla Channels (BCS)
- Tabwand Support Network (TSN)
- Career-Advancement and Women's Entrepreneurship Champions Organisation (CAWEECO)
- Women's Financial and Digital Inclusion education platforms (WFFIDI)
- Women's Entrepreneurship Day Organisation (WED)
- Men Should Lead Forum (MSL)
- Women's Leadership Arena Summit (WLAS)
- Berla Channels International Centre (BCIC) for Skills Development

These platforms serve as vehicles for capacity building and skill development, with a strong focus on gender equity and sustainable growth.

Dr. Yenwo is also a devoted wife, mother, and grandmother, whose life and work continue to inspire generations across Cameroon and beyond.

About the Publisher

Spears Books is an independent publisher dedicated to providing innovative publication strategies with emphasis on Africana stories and perspectives. As a platform for alternative voices, we prioritize the accessibility and affordability of our titles to ensure that relevant and often marginal voices are represented in the global marketplace of ideas. Our titles – poetry, fiction, narrative nonfiction, memoirs, reference, travel writing, African languages, and young people's literature – aim to bring African worldviews closer to diverse readers. Our titles are distributed in paperback and electronic formats globally by African Books Collective.

Connect with Us: Go to www.spearsbooks.org to learn about exclusive previews and read excerpts of new books, find detailed information on our titles, authors, subject area books, and special discounts.

Subscribe to our Free Newsletter: Be amongst the first to hear about our newest publications, special discount offers, news about bestsellers, author interviews, coupons and more!

Subscribe to our newsletter by visiting www.spearsbooks.org

Quantity Discounts: Spears Books are available at quantity discounts for orders of ten or more copies. Contact Spears Books at orders@spearsmedia.com.

Host a Reading Group: Learn more about how to host a reading group on our website at www.spearsbooks.org